Indian Perspectives on the U.S.
Literature and Foreign Affairs

In the same series

Jewish American Writers and Intellectual Life in America
D. Venkateswarlu

Jewish American Drama
D. Venkateswarlu

The Novels of William Styron
S. Laxmana Murthy

The Novels of Bernard Malamud
M. Rajagopalachari

Leaders in American Geography
Thomas F. Barton and *P.P. Karan*

Indian Perspectives on the U.S.

Literature and Foreign Affairs

Edited by

P.M. Kamath

A.A. Mutalik-Desai

Published by
Prestige Books
3/28, East Patel Nagar
New Delhi 110 008

ISBN: 81-85218-76-5

Phototypesetting by
Pivot Computers
Delhi 110 006
Ph. 291 8404

Printed at
Mehra Offset Press
New Delhi 110 002

Contents

Indian Perspectives on the U.S.: Literature and Foreign Affairs

A.A. MUTALIK DESAI and P.M. KAMATH

I

In the following nine essays on American literature in the twentieth century, certain thematic patterns and concerns emerge. From what is at first sight a mere welter of ideas, approaches, subjects and generalizations, a fairly cohesive and commonly held ground becomes visible. On the one hand, these essays are about a diverse and complex set of literary, humanist and philosophic questions: e.g., the contradictions and the paradoxes of the postbellum American South, the claims of Catholicism (as an institutionalized religion and a philosophic outlook on life), the African-American tidal wave of anger and indignation at all the past injustice and the continuing legacy of it, the vocal feminist resurgence, the perennial tug between the individual and his society, the irresolute dilemma between the ideal of freedom and the need for civilizational constraints, etc. But, on the other, through a seeming web of polarities, there is a search for meaning, order and resolution. With considerable justification one might state that these scholarly endeavours represent a pursuit of transcendence through, or even despite, conflict implicit in the reality of life. (Incidentally, with one exception, it is the modern American novel which is probed; and except in two cases, it is women writers—novelists and playwrights—who are studied!)

The fictional world of two relatively early twentieth-century women novelists, Willa Cather and Ellen Glasgow, is analyzed to reveal the constraints and contradictions of their time: the genteel, patriarchal traditions of the American South with its formal, false and affected aspects; the isolation of life; the incompatibility of life. And, yet, an assertion, a 'heroic' transformation through unflinching confrontation is in evidence. In Flannery O'Connor, too, there are strains and stresses: art and character, heaven and earth, concern for moral values and the path of violence. And, again, absolution or grace is not far off. Toni Morrison presents, perhaps appropriately, the bleakest and the most ambivalent vision: the two central characters in her landmark novel vanish into a transatlantic voyage or into misty swamps and dark forests. But, through tragedy and desolation, dreams are not altogether abandoned however distant and formidable it may be to realize them. Ann Petry, the other novelist of black plight and protest, exemplifies the 'mission-conscious' nature of contemporary African-American literature. The grim and desperate struggle does not portend any surrender. There is not even a hint of nihilism.

Norman Mailer, the quintessential post-World War II novelist, one who has always cast a weary and sceptical eye on the United States of his time, has nonetheless moved from conflict to clarity, from bewilderment to enlightenment or, at any rate, to an enlightened radical view of man and society. J.D. Salinger, another post-Second World War writer, focusses critical attention on the contemporary American society and castigates the adulation of Quiz-culture and valorizing of knowledge (as against wisdom) which cause psychic distortions, alienation and unhappiness. Ayn Rand, alone and unrepresentative, stands outside the American mainstream. The one essay on American theatre today explores the eco-feminist, experimental writing that goes well beyond traditional determinism. A possible affinity between American and Indian feminism is also fittingly suggested.

II

American foreign policy has always fascinated the Indian scholars both for its strength and weaknesses as a theoretical study. In the pre-independence period, American sympathetic attitude towards Indian freedom movement constituted a part of the U.S. foreign policy. Since independence, how America has used its power at different times with a view to enhance its ability to shape the course of international relations has drawn our attention. Until the disintegration of the Soviet Union and consequent end of the cold war, the U.S. policy-makers have used cold war tensions to heighten its policy-efficacy and if necessary in national interest, deemphasised cold war and promoted detente.

With the collapse of the Soviet Union, the U.S. alone is left in the international arena as a superpower, as a hegemon; emergence of its unchallenged status of hegemonic power has coincided with its relative decline as an economic power. This is of relevance to scholars in theory building but of immense concern to policy-makers. What are the economic instrumentalities the US as a "diminished giant" has been using to preserve its economic strength and how it is affecting India's vital interests could be seen in the analysis of issues like technology transfer, the US efforts to penetrate into newly industrialising countries and use of "Special 301" and "Super 301" provisions to enhance its economic interests. With the end of the cold war the economic interests have come to the forefront; but some of the cold war concerns in security areas have not disappeared. These have only been strengthened being buttressed by economic concerns. Here the issues relating to the Nuclear non-proliferation and human rights deserve a special attention.

III

The present anthology is a collection of selected papers presented at the 26th Annual Conference of the Indian Association for American Studies held at the M.S. University of Baroda in February 1992. A notable feature of the anthology is that it happily blends two important aspects of social sciences—literature and politics, for if literature records the hopes and aspirations of a nation, politics embodies its governing systems and attitudes to others. The present book therefore purports to be a mirror that reflects America's soul and no less her political philosophy and foreign affairs.

And finally we, on behalf of the IAAS, must place on record

our gratitude to Dr. R.K. Dhawan who has arranged to get the present volume published in such a short period, and so elegantly. Thanks are due to Dr. Suman Bala who, apart from handling the fiscal matters of the IAAS efficiently, took upon herself the task of an overview of this project and endeavoured to bring it out by the time of the 27th Annual Conference at Goa University. We are sure that this volume, addressed to a well-read and intelligent reader, will significantly enhance our understanding of the intrinsic value of American literature and help us to comprehend America's foreign policy which to many has been 'a hard nut to crack.'

Willa Cather and the New World Heroic

LAXMI PARASURAM

Critics have only belatedly realized the full significance of the fictional art of Willa Cather in its relation to the modernistic and American backgrounds within which she wrote. New biographical as well as recent critical insights into Cather's mind have somewhat revolutionised Cather criticism during the past two decades and these new critical approaches to Cather enable us to interpret her work in terms of a New World Heroic set in America and the modern world.

Earlier interpretations of Cather tended to relegate her position to that of a regional novelist. The nostalgic presence of a pioneer past in many of her well known novels often led to a critical view that she was backward looking, and the surface simplicity of her narrative mode and language seemed to deny her the privilege of being called a modernist. In spite of her depiction of heroic female characters who, like Earth Goddesses, turned the tides of history and the lives around them, Cather's attitude to gender was not considered radical enough to be on par with that of a modern feminist. Her treatment of ordinary reality as experienced by common people in strenuous frontier days was deemed more realistic than transcendent and the full measure of significance that Cather tries to bring out through her fictional works was mostly overlooked.

In recent appraisals of Cather's work, the deeper and more elusive qualities of her art are brought to our critical scrutiny. As early as in 1947, Maxwell Geismar had observed that Cather's is one of the most complex, difficult, and contradictory minds among our writers and it is this view that recent criticism has increasingly adopted to analyze the seeming simplicity of her themes and techniques and focus on their meaning and relevance to America and the modern world.

The most significant artistic achievement of Willa Cather, according to the present paper, is the heroic and archetypal dimension she brought on America's western experience. The transfiguration of history that Cather effected through creative memory and art gives us a new perspective not only on American, but on all human experience. Unlike many other writers in the modernist world who inveighed against the futility and anarchy of contemporary history, Cather looked at the whole of human history from the perspective of man's first confrontation with open spaces (as in the American frontier) and her novels expand the frontiers of the American west into a story of creation in which contact with the earth removes all data from history to leave only the basic thing: man's continuous fight to achieve something beyond himself. It is not Cather's use of Vergilian or pastoral traditions that brings distinct aura of grandeur and heroic dimension to Cather's frontier stories: what emerges in them as truly significant in a modern heroic sense is the series of self-transformations that Cather brings on human consciousness in the course of her novels to initiate a totally new way of perceiving reality. For Cather's protagonists, their confrontation with the formidable spaces in the frontier is a crucial experience—an experience that is akin to 'being dissolved into something complete and great' and this initiates in them a process of expansion of consciousness and reintegration with all the human past. This effect of magnification of ordinary lives through a revamping of consciousness in the course of settling a new country is what I would call the New World heroic which makes Cather's work unique in modern American literature.

The great fact in Cather's novels is the land itself which seems to overwhelm the little beginnings of human society that struggled in its sombre wastes. Jim Burden, her narrator in *My Antonia*, when faced with the barren open land of frontier Nebraska is at once overawed and says, 'there seemed to be nothing to see . . . there was nothing but land . . . not a country at all, but the material out of which countries are made. Between the earth and the sky, I felt erased, blotted out.' However, this initial experience of a total loss of identity leads Jim to an even more acute perception of the meaning of frontier experience not only in his own terms, but also of all immigrants. As Jim's childhood in Nebraska brings him close to many immigrant experiences, he establishes a particular bond of empathy with a Bohemian family whose various trials and tribulations in the new land initiate Jim to an understanding of a new value system that the land is made to reveal and represent. His memory of this frontier past in later life remains a precious incommunicable past and his view of Antonia, the Bohemian girl, is like that of a rich mine of life, of the founder of early races. The dull and ordinary life that Jim is obliged to live in the present is transfigured to something meaningful and unforgettable as he meets Antonia after 20 years and she comes to represent for him the country, the conditions and the whole adventure of his childhood.

Cather's characters are able to achieve varying measures of self-realisation through their confrontation with formidable open spaces of the frontier. Her character, Alexandra Bergson, in *O Pioneers* derives her epic strength and courage from the expanse of land around her. Her story is the story of human civilisation being shaped out of a land as flat and formless as the sea, and her final realisation in her own words is 'we come and go, but the land is always here. And the poeple who love it and understand it are the people who own it . . . for a little while.' Alexandra's insight about the land distinguishes her from her brothers who try to dominate the land, but fail miserably. Alexandra submits herself to the land knowingly and lovingly and then the Genius of the Divide, the great free spirit which breathes across it must have bent lower than it ever bent to a human will before. Alexandra shares spiritual communion with this Genius of the Divide, who, lover-like, Olympic in stature and redolent of harvest, gives her courage and tranquillity in spite of the great tragedy that overtakes her.

Cather's art transfigures the historic reality of the frontier to something archetypal and mythic and thus creates a new world heroic mode of dealing with nature and ordinary lives. Hers is an epic journey like that of her character, Thea, a journey from the confines of self and region to the universality of art and myth.

Cather as an artist is totally involved with modes of transforming the ordinary into the elemental or transcendent and she accords the status of a divine or heroic conqueror to the artist. Her artist conquerors work on common materials and are closely rooted on the earth. Thea, in *The Song of the Lark* gets ideas of art out of rocks, out of ancient relics and dead people, from the stream and broken jars of Panther Canyon. Art, according to her, reaches down to the procreative force of the earth and upto the heights of human yearning. Her quest for artistic perfection is a heroic quest for ideal beauty, and not a selfish quest for power and recognition. She responds to the summons from the world of art as to a call for a heroic action or sacred obligation and she is able to achieve the impossible and attain the realms of great art as a singer in spite of her lowly background and lack of sophisticated theories. It is a pure and simple idea of functionalism and closeness to the earth that enable an artist to achieve something great.

Cather's use of imagery and language testifies to the transfiguring features of her art. Some of her classical and Biblical allusions serve to elevate the struggles of her characters to heroic proportions as those of Aenias or Adam, but she most often makes use of the most common natural sights and phenomena to exalt the perceptions of her people and celebrate life and as they find them. In *My Antonia*, for example, Cather makes use of the celebrated image of the plough silhoutted against the setting sun to achieve a sense of glorious magnification of man's achievement in the world of nature. As Jim and the immigrant girls sit discussing why the Spanish explorer Coronado never went back to Spain, to his castles and riches, after discovering the American wilderness, they witness the magnificent scene of the setting sun, 'magnified across the distance by the horizontal light, it (the Plough) stood against the sun . . . black against the molten red. There it was, heroic in size, a picture writing on the sun.' Cather's art revels in images such as these that create symbolic meaning from natural phenomena. Similarly, Cather uses symbolic images of natural phenomena to sustain ideas of continuity, simultaneity, and cyclical pattern in historical changes. To sustain the meaning of the past in the present, Cather cites an instance of powerful planetary twinning of day and night in the appearance of the sun and the moon at the opposite edges of the world. A symbolic landscape and magical natural phenomena transmute Cather's everyday world into one of unusual grandeur and meaning.

Cather throws very interesting light on art and human history in terms of a transcendent awareness of man's life on earth. Amidst the Great Plains of American Mid-West Cather found a symbolic equivalent of the first beginning of human history and culture. Later when her novels dealt with areas like the American South-West where the relics of bygone ages and ancient civilisations are preserved in isolated spots, Cather is delighted to link the past and present and encompass a larger sweep of human history. Tom Outland in *Professor's House* finds that his excavations in Mesa Verde link him deeply to the perished tribe and he calls those ceramicists (whose pieces he has collected) 'my grandmothers'. Clearly, for Cather the past is neither exhausted or lost, but rather a vibrant reality lying at one's feet begging to be tapped so that it might bestow its precious secrets of continuity and meaning.

In her later book, *Death Comes for the Archbishop*, Cather takes up the mystic dimension of landscape and man's life on earth. The missionaries in the book are commissioned to carry the Cross into territories yet unknown and unnamed and they come to the vast expanses of New Mexico only to find an untamed land and people. But soon the land assumes a mystic significance, the world of men and the transcendent realm are closely connected and the ordinary reality acquires a numinous quality of the sacred. At the end, when Archbishop Latour prepares for death after a long life of service it is as though he were only completing the journey he had earlier undertaken. Latour had lived in the intersecting worlds of the pioneer and the mystic and past and future are woven together into a static continuous present in his consciousness which is informed by a vision of an eternal present. Therefore, he "sat in the middle of his own consciousness; none of his former states of mind were lost or outgrown. They were all within reach of his hand and all comprehensible." The Archbishop's death is only a natural transition to one state from another.

The vision of life and art that we find in Willa Cather is indeed unique, particularly for modern times. It is Cather's transcendental vision of earth and man that imparts such uniqueness to her work.

Burdwan University

The Polygamous Male: Ellen Glasgow's Protagonist in *The Romantic Comedians*

RAJYASHREE KHUSHU-LAHIRI

I had grown up in the yet lingering fragrance of the old South; and I loved its imperishable charm, even while I revolted from its stranglehold on the intellect.[1] This statement points to an essential aspect of Ellen Glasgow's life and art. Although as woman and as writer she managed to exist within the cultural and literary confines of the times, she yet lived and wrote as she wanted. She was certainly the first to revolt against the formal, the false, the affected in the Southern literary tradition of the time.[2] What the South needed most, she once said, was blood and irony. A realist, she looked at life around her with eyes that were neither clouded by sentiment nor veiled by romance. In her fiction, she was one of the first to strike a note of realism in Southern literature which was, until then, stepped for the most part in escapism and romanticism.

However, what she revolted against most, both in life and in art, was the restrictions society placed upon women. In the socio-cultural milieu in which she grew up, it was almost unimaginable for a woman to desire intellectual or professional fulfillment. Society conspired to thwart the mental development of a young girl. The education of a genteel lady comprised learning to read and write, a smattering of arithmetic, geography and history, with emphasis on deportment and fine arts. In short, she was groomed to fulfill the roles of a wife and mother. Ironically, an essential quality for being an ideal wife and mother was assumed to be a false innocence and ignorance about life.[3] The more ignorant a young girl was of the facts of life the better equipped she was considered to be able to deal with it. Over and over again, Ellen Glasgow in her novels has criticized the patriarchal society that conspires to produce this factitious purity and innocence—an unnatural state which proves to be inherently dangerous.

The lot of women, who were brought up to believe that their only aim in life was to make a suitable marriage, was not one to be envied. Glasgow gives a vivid description of the normal condition of womanhood:

> Women waiting for the first word of love from their lovers. Women waiting with all the inherited belief in the omnipotence of love, for the birth of their sons. . . . Women waiting beside the beds of the sick and dying—waiting—waiting.
>
> As a result I think it is almost impossible to overestimate the part that religion, in one form or another, has played in the lives of southern women. Nothing else could have made them accept with meekness the wing of the chicken and the double standard of morals.[4]

Early in life, Glasgow rebelled against this notion of womanhood when she decided to be a writer. Because of the hostility of her family towards her role as writer, her early work was written in secret to escape ridicule. In *A Certain Measure* she recalls: "When a bound copy of my first book reached me, I hid it under my pillow while a cousin, who had run in for breakfast, prattled beside my bed of the young men who had quarrelled over the privilege of taking her to Easter German."[5] It was not only her family that was not encouraging, but the attitude of the society in general was just as discouraging. The following incident she cites in her memoirs. *The Woman Within* is an example. When the manuscript of her first novel was completed, she took it to New York to be published. With great trepidation she approached Price Collier of the Macmillan publishing house, who took her to lunch but offered her no encouragement, rejecting the manuscript without reading it. "The best advice I can give you," he said with charming candour, 'is to stop writing, and go back to the South and have some babies.' And I think, though I may have heard this ripe wisdom from other men, probably from many, that he added: 'The greatest woman is not the woman who has written the finest book, but the woman who has had the finest babies'."[6] And when the novel, *The Descendant* was published, an elderly kinsman declared it to be incredible "that a well-brought-up Southern girl should even know what a bastard is."[7]

These personal experiences played an important role in shaping her personality and gave rise to her most persistent themes as a novelist. Maxwell Geismar describes her as 'a feminist with a vengeance.'[8] Unlike Edith Wharton, she was a self-acknowledged feminist, a suffragist who joined the Virginia League for Woman Suffrage. Twice she marched in suffrage parades; first in London with May Sinclair, and again in New York in 1911. She believed that 'suffrage for women is an inevitable fact in the social development of the race, and sentiment is as powerless to stay its coming as it is to stem the advancing tide of evolution.'[9] However, even though she evinced a certain interest in woman's suffrage, she was not deeply concerned with specifically feminine political goals, such as divorce, responsibility for and guardianship of children, inheritance rights, legal facilities denied to women, equal salaries, and so forth. Rather she was more interested in the intellectual and moral emancipation of women—in women's need for mental development and a life outside the emotions. This concern is inevitably translated into her fiction. It is best depicted in the weak and satirical portraits of the male protagonists who are advocates of the patriarchal culture norms, and the fundamental incompatibility between masculine and feminine expectations regarding the 'womanly woman' resulting in unsatisfactory man-woman relationships. The delineation of this theme is the concern of this paper.

The Romantic Comedians is the first novel in Glasgow's great trilogy of Richmond or "Queenborough." The other two are *They Stooped to Folly* and *The Sheltered Life*. The novels do not constitute a trilogy in the sense that they have a continuous plot or common characters. But, they share a common setting and class (the old but still prosperous Richmond families), and a spirit of ironic high comedy. They also share a hero, at least to the extent that the principal observer in each is an elderly man.

The Romantic Comedians is however, not pure comedy. Glasgow herself feared that the "ironic overtones" may seem to deny the tragic mood of the novel. For there is tragedy in the theme, though it is tragedy running, like the 'divine things' of Nietzsche, "on light feet." The novel is mainly centred in the consciousness of Judge Gamaliel Honeywell, a distinguished lawyer of aristocratic descent. And it is through his interactions with the two central female figures Amanda and Annabel that his character is delineated.

Unlike Jason in the *Barren Ground*, Honeywell is mocked rather than villainized. Through this satirical portrait Glasgow attacks the society that conveniently regards as "nature" in men what it considers "depravity" in women (7). The double standard of sexual morality that allows a sixty-six year old man to regard himself as a suitable mate for a twenty-three year old girl, whereas by common consent a fifty-eight year old woman must surely have put all thought of romance out of her head, is ironically debunked. Having written with bitterness of betrayed women who learned to live without the happiness of love, she now mocks the fatuous male who thinks polygamous happiness is his prerogative. Glasgow, writing about the theme of *The Romantic Comedians* says: 'As for the idea—well, I was worn out with having men write what they know or don't know about dangerous ages in women.'[10]

At the age of sixty-five, with the death of his wife Cordelia, Judge Honeywell begins to experience inexplicable but unmistakable longings in his autumnal years for a fulfillment which he had been denied in his youth. The novel opens with the Judge arranging lilies on his former wife's grave, surprised at the physical zest he felt after the year of mourning. Sitting beside the grave he sighs to himself that he is 'a bird with a broken wing,' only to find disconcertingly that 'his broken wing was helplessly trying to flutter.'[11] He feels youthful as compared to his friends. The memory of his ninety-year-old father, who had sired twelve children, and the sight of plethoric gentlemen of eighty foxtrotting on spindly legs make him feel 'that at sixty-five he was too young to renounce the innocent pleasures of life.' (72) Despite his confidence, and despite the 'budding and piping and twittering' (2) that is going on in his tempestuous heart, his person is subjected to close, harsh scrutiny. The author's eye does not spare the lean, stiff angularity, the brittle shanks, the veined and desiccated hands, the 'mottled stains under the eyes that flow into the sallow flush of the high cheek-bones, the corded folds of the throat.' (3)

Having got the 'maggot of youth' (134) into his head, he even deludes himself into believing that he does not look or feel a day older than thirty-five years. He feels remarkably young for his years, 'and after all—he had all tradition behind him in his opinion—a man is only as old as his instincts.' (49) Like other men he was polygamous by instinct; yet so far he had 'confined his impetuous desires within the temperate zone of monogamy.' (3) But now there is an "April burgeoning within" which draws him in the direction of sweet young girls, especially twenty-three-year old Annabel Upchurch, one of Cordelia's numerous poor cousins. His recurring sexual reveries are of Annabel's unclad limbs or of: 'the glimmering ivory shapes of nymphs, who danced on rose-white feet to the music of running water. In spirals and wreaths and garlands, faintly coloured like the earliest spring petals, they spun round him, whirling, drifting, flying, in the wind. . . . Clusters of girls, curving, swaying, bending, advancing, retreating, and always they smiled as they retreated, into the iridescent mist of April' (47). The daydream merges with an actual ball, in which flowerlike girls whirl beguilingly over the dance floor. His fantasies impel him toward the girls of twenty who are caught in the eddying dance, whereas public opinion seems to be firmly pushing him toward the past, toward queenly Amanda Lightfood.

Amanda, his first love and ideal, was the woman he had adored 'to the edge of delirium' in his early youth. She was then, and she remained for twenty years afterward, the crowned belle and beauty of Queenborough. Thirty-seven years ago, for a few blissful months, he had been engaged to her. But a lovers' quarrel had ended it, and while in pursuit of her on board a ship, the 'versatile emotions of man had entangled him in an affair with Cordelia' (13) and he had married her. Amanda's queenly pride had prevented her from making the smallest gesture of allurement or revealing by the slightest flicker of an eyelash that he had ruined her life. As the Judge reflected complacently, 'there was much to be said in favour of the womanly woman. At least men felt safe with her' (14). Secure in this thought, he could at times dwell sympathetically though ponderously upon her frustrated womanhood. 'It was, he felt, pathetic, it was even tragic, that she had never known the complete joy of belonging to some good man.' Indeed he was willing to make 'a heavy sacrifice in order to unite her to any good man in the world except himself' (34). Convinced that a man remains young longer than a woman of the same age, he cannot look upon Amanda as his contemporary, though she is eight years younger than him. For him, she is a well-preserved, grey-haired lady who must have put the thought of love outside of her life' (58). So far as he is concerned, beautiful women who were no longer young had ceased to interest him, and as he felt like a very young man, he considers it unfair that he should be assigned by the people about him to an elderly woman, and a spinster at that. And so, the more the society of Queenborough tried to push him in the direction of Amanda, the more determined he became every minute that he would refuse to be pushed.

In Amanda Lightfoot, Glasgow skilfully portrayed a woman completely formed by tradition. Somewhat laughably, yet pathetically, Amanda in the post-war age becomes a martyr to concepts of virtue and moral responsibility which have lost the universal respect of even her contemporaries. Almost forty years she has played the role of being Judge Honeywell's ideal, and has made a fetish of being faithful. She is quite divorced from reality, and despite the number of her ardent admirers in the past, she has no real knowledge of men. Annabel is quite right when she points out that women like Amanda have encouraged men to be 'morally flabby.' However, she really did not have much choice. Linda Wagner aptly comments: 'Taught to invest her life in the love of a good man, women like Amanda could only wait to be fulfilled.'[12] On the whole her situation provides genuine pathos. As Glasgow describes her: 'Serene, unselfish, with the reminiscence of a vanished day in her face and figure, she belonged to that fortunate generation of women who had no need to think, since everything was decided for them by the feelings of a lady and the Episcopal Church' (143).

The Judge's longing for youthful renewal instead of peace of mind, his fascination for 'the unwholesome, the prohibited, and the immoral' draws him toward Annabel. However, he always seeks to justify himself in terms of convention. Unwilling to admit his awakening passion for Annabel, he at first rationalizes his instinctive withdrawal from Amanda as a need to remain faithful to Cordelia's memory. Later, he complacently persuades himself that Annabel needs him more than he needs her. According to him, she requires not only his money and his kindness to recover from her disappointment in love, but, being a delicate woman he hopes that she may come to prefer his considerate caresses to the ardour of a youthful man. Moreover, he comically embroiders the actualities of Annabel's nature by continually relaxing the truth in her behalf: she is so pretty, he decides with passion instead of logic, that she cannot help being "good." He always thinks of her charm in terms of wild nature, of 'fields and streams,' of 'tall wind-blown grasses,' of the swallow's flight, of the 'April mist' in her gray-green eyes, and identifies her with the rose and ivory-coloured nymphs that trouble his imagination. He is unable to see how unsuited she is for the role of matron, especially as she is very free and completely devoid of moral duplicity. The contrast between her outward energy and her coldness toward him he interprets as a sign of maidenly reserve. Totally egocentric, he insists upon thinking of her as innocent and ignorant, and he even fatuously feels that he can mould her nature nearer to his ideal by being her perfect teacher. 'Training her tender mind had been, from the beginning of his engagement, one of the delights to which he had looked forward with deep satisfaction' (169). [13] That she is not the placid woman venerated by tradition and society and that she finds him physically repugnant, he fails to perceive for a long time. Masculine blindness and the evasive idealism of the culture which had formed him conspire to keep him ignorant of the truth, though there are moments when he wonders whether his own ideals of the opposite sex are mistaken. When it comes to understanding Annabel, his twin-sister Edmonia's injunction is certainly applicable: that 'the wisest man has only the wisdom of a fool when he tries to understand a woman' (87).

Annabel Upchurch, the protagonist, is an intelligent, unconventional and daring young woman. As the Judge realizes, she is 'delicate as a flower on the surface . . . but with a vein of iron beneath' (165). Determined to live her own life—her constant refrain is 'I want my life,'—and not be a 'sham'—she has no patience with hypocrisy and wonders what is so 'moral' about lying. She does not want to be a 'true' woman, i.e., conform to the conventional pattern of womanhood, because to her conventional women do not seem to be a bit 'real'. Fearlessly frank and outspoken, she makes no secret of her disappointment in love and the subsequent heart-break she suffers. She wonders how women of her mother's generation could 'keep alive with things like this bottled up inside of them. If they never talked of them and Mother says they would have died first, they must have let themselves be eaten away in secret' (110). Her unhappy affair with Angus Blount leads her to react adversely towards young men, whom she says she despises, and towards love and romance in general. Naively assuming that money could be a substitute for love, she is tempted to accept the Judge's proposal of marriage. However, her sense of justice and her honesty lead her to question Amanda about her feelings for the Judge before she accepts the proposal. Despite her strong desire to escape from genteel poverty, she 'wouldn't take a man away from another woman . . . if he were as rich as Croesus' (131).

Within a few months of her marriage to the Judge, she realises her folly, and how 'immoral' such a marriage can be. Her love for Dabney Birdsong only expedites the denouement. In an impassioned scene she blames her mother and the Judge for taking advantage of her innocence and ignorance about life and propelling her into an 'immoral' marriage. The vein of iron in her, will not allow her to be subdued and in spite of her mother's and husband's implorings, she elopes with Dabney. Mrs. Upchurch reflecting upon the disastrous outcome of her daughter's marriage and voicing the opinion of her society, is inclined to blame Annabel: 'In the earlier generations, how many girls had married men old enough to be their fathers or grandfathers, and yet nothing disastrous had come out of it, nothing at least, with which husbands, aided by duty or the fear of living, had not been able to deal. Women had known then how to live without love, just as they had known how to live without beauty or happiness' (300). However, the author's sympathies are with Annabel who escapes any real criticism for her actions. Not only does she allow her to live her own life, but she lets her find love and happiness.

In the end, it is the Judge who emerges as the most ridiculous and pathetic figure in the novel. In Judge Honeywell's prostration of himself before Annabel, there is indignity and morbidity. Mrs. Upchurch's view of the Judge dominates in the novel: 'Could anything, she asked herself, be more unmanly than an elderly man in the clutch of an emotional crisis?' (277) One would have expected that the debacle of his relationship with Annabel would have had a sobering influence on him. But after a period of illness, we see him on the verge of committing the same folly once again. The sight of the cool and fresh young nurse stirs up the same desires, and his last thought is: 'Spring is here, and I am feeling almost as young as I felt last year' (346).

Through the characterization of Judge Honeywell, Glasgow gives vent to her wrath, and seeks to puncture and punish the vanity of the patriarchal male. Her ironic sense of the disparity existing between the conventional views that men have regarding women, and the reality (which gives rise to serious problems in man-woman relationships) is given effective expression in this novel. Glasgow's ideal male figure would certainly be devoid of the double standards (that allow a man to fall in love even with one foot in the grave, but debar a woman from giving expression to her emotional needs) and the vanity which are so evident in Gamaliel Honeywell and are the product of a patriarchal culture.

NOTES

1. Ellen Glasgow, *A Certain Measure* (New York: Harcourt, Brace, 1938), p. 12.
2. Maxwell Geismar, *Rebels and Ancestors: The American Novel, 1890-1915* (Boston: Houghton Mifflin, 1953), p. 219.
3. Reference may be made to Edith Wharton's novels, especially *The Age of Innocence* where she strongly criticizes this. Glasgow's novel *The Sheltered Life* also provides a similar critique.
4. Cited in Linda W. Wagner, *Ellen Glasgow: Beyond Convention*

(Austin: University of Texas Press, 1982), p. 4.
5. Glasgow, *A Certain Measure*, p. VII.
6. Ellen Glasgow, *The Woman Within* (New York: Harcourt, Brace, 1954), p. 108.
7. Glasgow, *A Certain Measure*, p. 9.
8. Geismar, p. 220.
9. Note, dated 1910 in Glasgow Papers, quoted in E. Standly Godbold, *Ellen Glasgow and the Women Within* (Baton Rouge: Louisiana State University Press, 1972), p. 92.
10. Glasgow, *Letters*, p. 90. Quoted in Wagner, p. 83.
11. Ellen Glasgow, *The Romantic Comedians* (New York: A.L. Burt Company, 1926), p. 1. All further references to the book will be incorporated in the text.
12. Wagner, p. 93.
13. Reference may be made to Edith Wharton's heroes who exhibit a similiar desire.

M.G. Science Institute
Gujarat University
Ahmedabad

Flannery O'Connor and Catholic Dogmatism

S. KANAKRAJ

Among the fiction-writers of today, Flannery O'Connor occupies a unique place. By working theological and philosophical subtleties into the structure of her tales and by fusing the transcendent world with the sublunary one, she makes heaven come down and walk on the earth. Her life was short, her experience of the world limited and her total output small, but in her slender volume of fiction one finds a fairly wide range of episodes and incidents and an amazing variety of characters. Besides her fictional work, there are two volumes, one entitled *Mystery and Manners* (1969), a collection of her occasional prose articles and her lectures, and the other, *Habit of Being* (1979), a collection of her letters, both published posthumously, which give the reader a deep insight into her personality and world-view.

Early in her life (1950), she was stricken with lupus, the dreaded disease that was to carry her away 14 years later. During this period, her natural cheerfulness and strength of character enabled her to endure her affliction. Being devoutly religious, she surrendered herself completely to God when she became aware of the proximity of death. As Dorothy McFarland says:

> More than most catholics . . . she was faced early with the necessity of preparing for death and this fact is surely related to the importance that death assumes in her fiction—it is not hard to see some connection between this and the terrifying aspect the transcendent often assumes in her stories.[1]

The will to be a writer was so strong that nothing could make her desist. Added to this, she was a perfectionist and spent a lot of time, revising, rewriting and polishing her work to the annoyance of her agent and publisher. On top of it all, she was endowed with a laudable critical intelligence, so that her artistic development was quite rapid. She worked with a sense of urgency to the very end, which came in 1964. Thus passed away, in the prime of her life and career, a woman of rare bravery, an artist of superb talent to join that select group of 'inheritors of unfulfilled renown,' in the words of Shelley.

Flannery O'Connor allowed her Catholic orthodoxy to influence every piece of her writing. When a critic ignores this aspect of O'Connor's fiction, his assessment tends to go awry. This is exactly what happens in the case of Josephine Hendin's analysis and evaluation of O'Connor as artist. Hendin prefers to avoid the heavily theological enquiry pursued by most other critics and the result is an incompleteness in the critic's assessment. Hendin's conclusion is that 'O'Connor's assertions of Christian orthodoxy do not accurately desscribe her art. They are belied by the human experience in her work.'[2] Similarly, Maya Tugusheva considers the religious sections of the stories to be mere trappings. She says that in the best of O'Connor's stories social realism succeeds in suppressing religious dogma. 'O'Connor's submission to Catholicism and her penchant for realism, co-exist amiably, only to a certain point. Often the realistic approach manages to break loose from the Procrustean bed of dogma . . . such a contradictory position and a victory over dogma are evident in her best stories.'[3]

All this is to ignore what is so very obvious to the readers and to most of the critics, namely, that all her stories are about the operations of Divine Grace in the lives of ordinary men and women. Salvation comes in strange and unexpected ways which are so delicate that the best minds may miss them completely. At the very start of her career O'Connor committed herself implicitly to the Christian theme and pursued it with devotion till the end. In "The Fiction Writer and His Country" she wrote, 'I see from the standpoint of Christian orthodoxy. This means that for me the meaning of life is centered in our Redemption by Christ.'[4] And she plays exquisite variations on this central theme of Redemption through Grace. She proceeds from the doctrine of Man's Fall and depicts his fallen state in a large gallery of characters, who are proud, humble, mean, magnanimous, intolerant, ignorant, grasping and greedy. To each one of them is offered the opportunity of salvation, which comes in strange and often unexpected ways. Those who perceive it and accept it are saved, even at the point of death. Those who ignore and reject the opportunity are doomed.

God's love for man was expressed through Christ's death on the cross. 'God so loved the world that He gave His only begotten Son, that whosoever believeth in Him should not perish, but have everlasting life' (John 3:16). Acceptance of this love is called Grace. Grace is supernatural; it is above man's natural sphere of life and he may accept or reject the offer.

The pattern of redemption is a progress, a movement from the condition of sinfulness through contrition, confession, penance and absolution. In the novels, the full course is traced in detail, but in the short stories such protraction is not possible. Recognition and acceptance of grace or rejection of it can only take a short time. Most of her short stories are constructed in such a way as to dramatize the sinfulness and the need for grace, followed by, near the end of the story, an epiphany in which the main character recognises his need for repentance and either accepts or ignores the opportunity. The acceptance of grace may be, in some cases, during a sudden revelation, even at the moment of violent death as in the case of Mrs. May, the heroine of 'Greenleaf,' the old lady who is gored to death by a bull, or Grandmother, the heroine of the masterpiece, 'A Good Man is Hard to Find' who is shot to death brutally by an escaped convict. Epiphany may come even through trifling things as the water-stain in 'Enduring Chill,' the plaster-of-paris effigy in 'The Artificial Nigger' or the setting sun resembling the Eucharist in the monstrance.

In the case of a large number of persons, epiphany follows experiences dominated by pride, sin, godlessness etc. Asbury Fox in 'Enduring Chill,' Mrs. Turpin in 'Revelation,' Julian in 'Everything that Rises' and Parker in 'Parker's Back'—all of them experience this kind of epiphany. Asbury's agnosticism, intellectual superiority and self-righteous liberalism succumb to the implacable descent of the Holy Ghost seen in the water-stain. O'Connor shows the operation of grace from many different angles. Whether she indicated it through direct statement or by subtle revelation of an interior condition she leaves little question that she means for her readers to apprehend the moment of grace as surely as her characters do.

That her view of life is essentially religious has been agreed upon by almost every critic. 'All of O'Connor's works are concerned with Christian values, even though some of her short stories do not touch upon religion directly.'[5] Even her criminals and misfits are close to salvation because they are fighting a spiritual battle within themselves. What puzzles critics and readers alike is the use she makes of violence and brutality in her fiction. For example in 'A Good Man is Hard to Find,' the Misfit and his companions wipe out a whole family in the most casual manner. After listening to this tale, Van Wyke Brooks remarked that 'it was a shame one with so much talent should look upon life as a horror story.'[6] O'Connor's reaction to such criticism was clearly and categorically voiced in a letter she wrote to her friend "A":

> I am mighty tired of reading reviews that call 'A Good Man is Hard to Find' brutal and sarcastic. The stories are hard, but they are hard because there is nothing harder or less sentimental than Christian realism. I believe that there are many rough beasts slouching toward Bethlehem to be born and that I have reported the progress of a few of them.[7]

Defending the apparently brutal nature of her fiction, she wrote:

> in my own stories I have found that violence is strangely capable of returning my characters to reality and preparing them to accept their moment of grace. . . . It is the extreme situation that best reveals what we are essentially.[8]

Having committed herself to writing on the religious theme of redemption through grace, at the start of her career she remained loyal to her commitment till the end:

> She pursued it with persistence and devotion until her death. Any attempt at an appreciation of her work must begin with a clear understanding of this. . . . She fuses the transcendent world with the sublunary one, achieving such a convergence of actualities that one is meaningless without the other.[9]

Critics should keep this in mind if they wish to avoid the crime of missing the most important point.

Of course, Flannery O'Connor was not a preacher, propagating any religion. She was primarily an artist who had chosen to express her vision through fiction. As Josephine Hendin says:

> To assume as some critics do, that her work is merely a monologue on redemption, is to see it only in part to ignore much of its meaning and to lose sight of the believer, behind the belief. My own feeling is that O'Connor never merely wrote about redemption, but that the very act of writing was itself a redemptive process for her. It may have been the only, and perhaps the unconscious way she could express all the contradictions within her. . . . I do not think that O'Connor's fiction can be explained by her Catholicism alone.[10]

Though religion is the major theme of her fiction, one should not expect religion or morality to be central to every story:

> All of the stories are not religion oriented. Some few . . . are religious only in the broadest sense. . . . Others lend themselves readily to analysis through religious terminology. . . . Nearly all the other stories may be categorised on the basis of their open concern with religious themes.[11]

O'Connor was first and foremost an artist and

> the artist has his hands full and does his duty if he attends to his art. He can safely leave evangelising to the evangelists.[12]

O'Connor, as an artist was aware of the duty of the artist. In a letter to Shirley Abbot, she says:

> I write with a solid belief in all the Christian dogmas. . . . I don't write to bring anybody a message, as you know yourself that this is not the purpose of the novelist, but the message I find in the life I see is a moral message.[13]

On one side we have critics like sister M. Bernetta Quinn who believes that every story embodies a sacrament and like Robert Drake who claims that O'Connor saw herself as an evangelist who had come to call the wicked to repentance. On the other side, there are critics like Maya Tugusheva who considers theology to be mere drapery in the stories and like Josephine Hendin who downplays the importance of the religious theme. A level-headed critic like Irving Howe sees O'Connor's orthodoxy as only one aspect of her work. Actually there is no getting away from the fact that whatever the motif of her story may be, the major theme is always man's fallen condition and his redemption through the grace of God. A reliable critic like Dorothy Walters accepts O'Connor's theological basis and examines the stories from that standpoint. Her assessment is something that can be accepted by most readers and critics.

> She is undeniably a craftsman of the first rank, her work exerts a forcefulness of appeal associated with only the highest talents. Above all she is characterised by absolute integrity of vision and craft. Indeed it seems safe to predict that her work will endure as long as the art of the story teller is valued by society and as long as such things as stories exist.[14]

Robert Coles concludes his study of her fiction with a brilliant paradox stating that O'Connor was "a soul blinded by faith, hence with an uncanny endowment of sight."[15]

NOTES

1. Dorothy Tuck MacFarland, *Flannery O'Connor* (New York: Frederick Ungar, 1976), pp. 7, 8.
2. Josephine Hendin, *The World of Flannery O'Connor* (Bloomington: Indiana University Press, 1970), p. 16.
3. Maya Tugusheva, "The Most American Genre" in *20th Century American Literature: A Soviet View* (Moscow: Progress Publishers, 1976), p. 135.
4. Flannery O'Connor, *Mystery and Manners*, ed. Sally and Robert Fitzgerald (New York: Farrar, Strauss and Girowc, 1969), p. 32.
5. Patricia D. Maida, "Light and Enlightenment in Flannery O'Connor's Fiction" in *Studies in Short Fiction*, Winter 1976, p. 34.
6. Flannery O'Connor, *Habit of Being*, ed. Sally Fitzgerald, p. 85.
7. *Ibid.*, p. 90.
8. Flannery O'Connor, *Mystery and Manners*, pp. 112, 113.
9. Carter W. Martin, *The True Country: Themes in the Fiction of Flannery O'Connor* (Nashville: Vanderbilt University Press, 1969), p. 9.
10. Josephine Hendin, p. 17.
11. Carter W. Martin, pp. 21, 22.
12. Flannery O'Connor, *Mystery and Manners*, p. 171.
13. Flannery O'Connor, *The Habit of Being.*
14. Dorothy Walters, *Flannery O'Connor* (New York: Twayne, 1973), p. 21.
15. Robert Coles, *Flannery O'Connor's South* (Baton Rouge: Louisiana State Univ. Press, 1980), p. 161.

ICC & CE
M.K. University
Madurai

Conflicting Claims in Toni Morrison's Novels: Realism vs. Fantasy, Aesthetic Verisimilitude vs. Captious Ethnic Pride

A.A. MUTALIK-DESAI

> Realism is 'concerned with giving a truthful impression of actuality as it appears to the normal human consciousness.'
>
> Vivian de Sola Pinto

> Blacks are 'some of the most complicated, interesting, mysterious people in the world.' Toni Morrison

What is the state of realism in contemporary American fiction? American literature produced the novels of Theodore Dreiser, Upton Sinclair, Sinclair Lewis and others not too long ago and more recently John Steinbeck's *The Grapes of Wrath* (1939), Norman Mailer's *The Naked and the Dead* (1948), James Jones' *From Here to Eternity* (1951), Truman Capote's *In Cold Blood* (1965) and Saul Bellow's *The Dean's December* (1982) now seems to question the very meaning and the role of realism. As an example of this emerging phenomenon, I wish to examine in this essay the first four novels of Toni Morrison.

Morrison is not just another black[1] novelist. She is a remarkable American novelist. She is an intellectual in her own right. She is a vital part of the black community's avant-garde. Her views count. What she thinks earns a following. Therefore, initially, here, her thoughts on the race relations in the U.S. deserve to be stated. These will also be a preface to my discussion. Let me use three quotations. 1) One of her earliest memories growing up in the middle-western state of Ohio is about her grandfather's pessimism drilled into her, as it turned out. He, a youth at the time of the Emancipation Proclamation, 'was . . . convinced that there was no hope whatever for black people in this country.'[2] 2) 'I grew up in a basically racist household with more than a child's share of contempt for white people.'[3] 3) Her own assessment of the white vs. black context is quite revealing: 'my hatred of white people is justified and their hatred for me is not.'[4]

In a society where blue eyes and blond hair epitomize the ultimate in beauty, Pecola in *The Bluest Eye* (1970) has neither, of course. A black girl in a predominantly white society, she is familiar with the dictum: 'if you are white you are all right; if you are brown you can stick around; but if you are black . . . get back.' So she dreams everyday for the impossible:

> It had occurred to Pecola sometime ago that if her eyes, those eyes that held the pictures, and knew the sights—if those eyes of hers were different, that is to say, beautiful, she herself would be different. Her teeth were good, and her nose was not big and flat like some of those who were thought so cute. . . . Pretty eyes, Pretty eyes, Pretty blue eyes, Big blue pretty eyes. . . . Each night, without fail, she prayed for blue eyes.[5]

Pecola's dream cannot be realized. Her life is assailed by poverty, desperation, incest and humiliation. She cannot distinguish between the subliminal and the symbolic desire for beauty through blue eyes and the actuality of it. The constraints of life, both from within and without, break her and her disintegration becomes a visible fact. Her desire is her tragic nemesis, even as the same desire is indicative of the cultural and racial realities of life in the U.S. It must be pointed out, and not merely incidentally, that the novelist does not address herself to the more basic question whether white America is somehow imposing a set of values on a minority of her people who are long dispossessed or are the blacks themselves to blame for adopting the ways of the whites too readily, and thus failing to guard their own individual and collective self. As at least one critic has averred, Morrison's *The*

Bluest Eye is really about 'the conflict of artistic and societal values between the Anglo-American and Afro-American cultures. . . . As such, this novel is about mythic, political, and cultural mutilation as much as it is a book about race and sex hatred.' While this view may be endorsed, Morrison does not deal with the theme (namely: an innocent, impressionable black girl snared by certain Western or Nordic concepts of physical beauty) on a realistic plane or within the range of verisimilitude. A theme that lends itself to a sociological nexus is here treated with a touch of fantasy and surrealism, and the narrative goes astray amidst rhythms of jazz or the changing seasons of nature! Does this square with the novelist's stated purpose of capturing the specificity of black culture?[6] But *The Bluest Eye* is only a prologue to the yet more uneven and strident discourse to follow.

Sula (1974) picks up where the first novel left off. Sula, the protagonist, must obviously face the same social and cultural *milieu*: racial prejudice, sexism, the need for conformity and the overwhelming hypocrisy in a small middle-western town. As before, a bond between two females is employed to project the paradoxes and the ironies of life. If Pecola had *her* obsession, Sula has *hers*:

> [She] lived out her days exploring her own thoughts and emotions, giving them full reign, feeling no obligation to please anybody unless their pleasure pleased her. As willing to feel pain as to give pleasure, hers was an experimental life. . . . She had no center. . . . She was completely free of ambition, with no affection for money, no greed, no desire to command attention or compliments—no ego.[7]

Her own thoughts and emotions. No obligations. No centre. No desire. No ego. Morrison's characters would not be complete without paradox and contradiction deeply ingrained in them. But, whether it is Pecola or Sula, what sets the reader on edge is not so much the hyperbole invested in the characters or the situations. It is rather the novelist's dour, unrelenting, unequivocal and even simplistic ideas on the question of white vs. black America. So much so that the final outcome of a novel points to a basic flaw in Morrison's vision of life. An example: Scornfully she has equated any determined struggle towards respectability with white middle-class values. Therefore, upward mobility is suspect. As Carol Ianone has commented, 'There is a strain in her thought which seems not only not to condemn but even to endorse certain pathological elements in black life. . . . "They [the blacks] may be in prison, [but] they are adventurous . . . the fact that they would split in a minute just delights me. It's part of the whole business of breaking ground."'[8] Such observations are not casually dropped. They form a continuing *motif* in her work. The same crabby and captious attitude is almost habitual and for it realism or even credibility is jettisoned and the novel is used, without any hesitation, as a pulpit. *Sula* is only yet another example in which Morrison's black consciousness prevails at the expense of aesthetic and literary probability and intellectual probity.

Song of Solomon (1977) has, as a departure, a male protagonist, untiring in his efforts at material prosperity and acquisition. He is Macon. His surname is 'Dead.' His nickname is 'Milkman.' The hospital where he was born is 'No Mercy Hospital.' The street on which he lives is named 'No Doctor Street.' Others in this novel have names like 'Pilate' and 'Guitar.' The structure and the substance of Macon's story is based on two conflicting sides: his need for matters earthy on the one hand and for matters etheral (literally!) on the other. More so than the first two novels, *Song of Solomon* is part picaresque and part fable in form and points to the way Morrison's work may be heading—which is an increasing emphasis on myth and fantasy, fable and allegory and a radical departure from, indeed abandonment of, any concern for 'giving a truthful impression of actuality.'

By 1981 Toni Morrison had reached a decisive stage in her career. Looking back on the three novels published between 1970 and 1977, one finds a pattern, a repetition of themes such as search for beauty (more physical than transcendent), the American South vs. North dichotomy, an acute class consciousness, mundane boredom vs. spiritual emptiness, a preoccupation with the plight of black women, etc. Against this background, we may now turn to *Tar Baby* (1981).

Thematically, *Tar Baby* is not only diverse and complex, it is also a throwback to *The Bluest Eye*, *Sula* and *Song of Solomon*. But as a novel of 'plight and protest' (in the words of Irving Howe), *Tar Baby* is a special case.

Somewhere in the Caribbean there is an island by name Isle des Chevaliers. On it there is a house by name L'Arbe de la Croix. It is designed by Mexicans. It is built by Haitian labourers. In it resides a slightly eccentric, tired, disenchanted, seventyish, entirely benevolent (even indulgent) white American, Valerian Street. He leads the good life. He has all the money in the world, having retired as candy manufacturer. He is married to a former Beauty Queen. He carefully tends to his greenhouse plants. He listens to the music of Chopin, Bach, Haydn and Listz while sipping his wine. A most faithful and efficient pair of housekeepers (a black couple, Sidney and Ondine Childs) wait on him to cater to his slightest wishes and to indulge him in his whims and vagaries. He has it made. In all this perpetual bliss he hopes to 'saunter toward . . . [his] . . . last and final hour.' That wish is not going to be fulfilled so readily.

Among those around him is his wife Margaret, almost a generation younger. She lives in a world apart. Once, still in the bloom of her youth and beauty, she felt that motherhood had come too early, almost an imposition. She hated the baby. It is now that she would like to baby him and make up for the past in a manner of atonement to ease her anguish and allay her guilt. She hopes that her son will come home for Christmas. That wish is not going to be fulfilled so readily either.

The elderly black retainers are more like family and so is their orphaned niece Jadine, Valerian having arranged for her education which has helped her to become a chic fashion model and an urbane, elegant, haughty, assertive individualist. Having graduated from the high fashion world of New York and Paris, she is taking stock of her life. Here on this enchanted island and the blessed house, in the midst of wine and music, the adoring presence of her uncle and aunt and the civilized and melancholy and engagingly cynical conversations with Valerian, she would like to chart a course for her future: a wish that is not at all going to be fulfilled.

That is the setting of *Tar Baby*, with conflict implicit and tragic consequences lurking dangerously close to the surface. Much to Margaret's dismay her son Michael does not come home for Christmas. Her distress and her long-suppressed rage shatter the idyllic and dreamy world of L'Arbe de la Croix. A word of bickering here and an indiscreet remark there result into a fight between Margaret and Ondine and it leads to tragic revelations. A gay and convivial Christmas dinner ends in pain and remorse for all. No one's prayer is answered. No one's wish is fulfilled. Ghosts from Christmases past come to haunt, and they leave in their trail a heap of broken dreams.

But, even before these climactic scenes are enacted, another crucial member of *Tar Baby* is introduced. He is William Green alias Herbert Robinson alias Louis Stover alias Son! His appearance in Jadine's life is a dramatic and devastating turn: for her and, indirectly, for everyone in the story. If there was ever an odd couple, a most incompatible pair, this is one. She is the cool sophisticate, chic to her shining finger nails. He is the primitive incarnate. She quotes Henry David Thoreau. He talks *ad infinitum* of his life among the country bumpkins in a godforsaken place called Eloe in the backwoods of Florida. Yet they fall for each other. If their loving is a soothing potion, their fighting is a deadly poison. Jadine soon knows that she must leave him, which she eventually does . . . unceremoniously. He follows her, pursues her across land and water, across swamp and forest. All of which ends shrouded in mystery. Prompted and lead by the enigmatic and blind Therese, he makes his way towards the legendary horsemen and their elusive women of the island to be lost among them forever. Or, that is what one is left to surmise.

In this otherwise languid and highly readable tale of romance and mystery, clearly etched characters and sparkling dialogue, Morrison is driven compulsively to entertain once again her *idee fixe*, her perceptions of the relationships between whites and blacks, and to recall the American past which is one of bitter and acrimonious heritage and the present which, according to this novelist at any rate, only points to more of the same: shouting across an insurmountable barrier and looking at one another uncomprehendingly—hardened as both sides are by memories of shame and disgust, hatred and mistrust. In the first three novels

Morrison had raised the banner of black pride and had sounded the note of 'plight and protest,' and quite justifiably so. Even in those novels, however, it is a case not only of Black-Is-Beautiful but also one that explicitly states that all the rest is ugly. The traumas of Pecola, Sula and Macon are seen in terms which are all white or all black. Gray areas which usually dominate life's vast canvas totally disappear in her radical, absolute blackness and whiteness of men and women and things. In *Tar Baby*, the shrill, undigested and ill-balanced protest reaches a new hysterical pitch. Consider the following:

William Green, i.e., Son, is a black drifter, a self-made social outcast, a man wanted by several law enforcement agencies (for willful deception, deserting his post on board a ship, criminal trespass, violence and, perhaps, murder) is now provided with shelter and protection by the white host, Valerian Street, all the legal and other transgressions notwithstanding! An extraordinary situation and an extraordinary act of generosity. But when this host dismisses his own servants for conduct unbecoming (namely, theft and pilferage), it is Son of all persons who begins to wonder if Valerian's action isn't the worst example of a white man's colonial, imperialist, exploitative, slave-owning mentality. Quite promptly Morrison sets up Son as the moral arbiter:

> he [Valerian] had been able [Son thinks] to dismiss with a flutter of the fingers the people whose sugar and cocoa had allowed him to grow old in regal comfort; although he had taken the sugar and cocoa and paid for it as though it had no value [whatever that means], as though the cutting of cane and picking of beans was child's play and had no value. . . . In the meanwhile this one here would chew a morsel of ham and drink white wine secure in the knowledge that he had defecated on two people [the two servants who had been dismissed] who had dared to want some of his apples.[9]

Such vacuous and untenable rhetoric! In the same breath the altogether benign white host is equated with polluters, killers, slave-drivers and the lowest scum. Morrison's crabby, vitriolic, aggressive and racist credo is nowhere better illustrated than in *Tar Baby*. Those who are most indebted, personally, to Valerian

Street are by some perverse reckoning given the most caustic words to hurl at him. Valerian is to be condemned, it seems, because, after all, what has he upheld except such material commitments like industry; whereas Son is to be lionized as he has upheld the ideal of fraternity. In the context of the novel (and the particular situation in it), none of this makes any sense. One is reminded of the absurdity of the court-room scene in Bertolt Brecht's play *The Caucacian Chalk Circle* in which a witness *still in the witness box* berates the presiding magistrate himself! Morrison's rhetoric of racial pride easily outdoes Brecht's rhetoric of socialism and the exploitation of the proletariat.

There are other instances too of the same muddle and miasma: Son refuses to attend a college of law because he doesn't 'want to know their laws; I want to know mine.' He doesn't want any education given by white America for that education is not about *him*. He admonishes Jadine expertly:

> The truth is that whatever you learned in those colleges . . . didn't include me. . . . What did they teach you about me? . . . Did they tell you what I was like, did they tell you what was on my mind? Did they describe me to you? Did they tell you what was in my heart? If they didn't teach you that, then they didn't teach you nothing, because until you know about me, you don't know nothing about yourself.[10]

And so on and so forth, *ad nauseum*. While there is a point in a black man demanding education which includes his history, heritage and culture, Morrison is scating on thin ice as the tone is too clearly one of us vs. them. If the portrait of Jadine is a reminder to blacks who forgot their own roots, their 'ancient properties' and are content with succeeding in the white society playing the white man's game as it were, then the simplistic, sophomoric and woolly notions of Son are ultimately destructive. As one reviewer cautiously suggested, there is something ominous here.

Let it be said without any equivocation that Toni Morrison possesses the rare talents and skills a novelist needs. Her stories (despite occasional flaws) come alive. Characters are vivid and memorable. Dialogue is varied, rich and intense. But Toni Morrison the black, female activist and intellectual makes her works vehicles of much—and much that is too steeped in anger to be objective, too one-sided to achieve artistic and aesthetic credibility. When asked by an interviewer, Thomas LeClair, about these considerations, she has responded dismissively, saying, 'This kind of sociological judgment [of her novels] is pervasive and pernicious. . . . Unforgivable.'[11]

The inscription to *Tar Baby* is a quotation from *I Corinthians* (1-11): 'For it hath been declared unto me of you, my brethren, by them which are of the house of Chloe, that there are contentions among you.' Morrison's novels are indeed contentious.

NOTES

1. Well within one's living memory, there has been a perceptible if also somewhat curious series of changes in how one should refer to the major non-white population of the U.S. Dismissing off-hand those many impolite, snickering, brazen and downright demeaning terms, one begins with the appellation 'negro.' Then came 'coloured' during the 1950s at the time of the first social and political thrust since World War II to undo centuries' old injustice. By the mid-1960s 'blacks' became the preferred expression. Since then it was 'Afro-American' for a while and currently, as the weather vane would have it, it is 'African-American.' In this essay the term 'black' or 'blacks' is retained mainly because that is the usage found in Morrison's writing.
2. Carol Iannone, 'Toni Morrison's Career,' *Commentary*, December, 1987, p. 60.
3. *Ibid.*
4. Thomas LeClair, 'The Language Must Not Sweat,' *New Republic*, 21st March 1981, pp. 26-29.
5. *The Bluest Eye* (New York: Holt, Rinehart and Winston, 1970), p. 40.
6. Iannone, p. 60.
7. These sentiments are *stated*. But it is not evident if they are *realized* in the novel.
8. Iannone, p. 61.
9. *Tar Baby* (London: Triad/Granada, 1982 reprint), pp. 203-5.
10. *Ibid.*, p. 267.
11. LeClair, as above.

I.I.T., Bombay

Fiction as a Weapon of Protest: Ann Petry's *The Street*

AMINA AMIN

Black writers have from the beginning written a literature of protest and black women have always cried out against injustice. As far back as in 1772 Phillis Wheatley had expressed her anguish at being snatched from her parents' homeland and made a slave. The first America-born woman to speak in public was black. In the early 1800s and the beginning of the 20th century black women writers, poets and novelists continued to assert the humanity of black women.

Slave narrative appeared in rudimentary form during the latter part of the 1700s and continued to be written till 1865 when it reached its full development as a special genre of black writing. These narratives were written primarily to draw the attention of the world towards the oppression of the black people by their masters. Slave narratives played the role of anti-slavery literature triggering the Abolition Movement. Slave narratives and black fiction developed along similar lines. To quote Clavin C. Hernton:

> The cross-fertilization between the slave-narrative and the black novel is an important part of what goes to make up the black literary tradition.[1]

In other words, there is a generic relationship between slave narratives and black fiction for both portray a succession of episodes, incidents and passages of moral outcry against the cruelty, violence and oppression of the blacks by the whites. Thus, as Calvin Hernton rightly observes:

> By virtue of its origin, nature and function, black-writing is

mission-conscious.[2]

Richard Wright's *Native Son* (1940) became the first black novel to depict realistically and naturalistically the effects of racism and capitalism on black males in the American urban ghetto environment. In many ways Ann Petry's *The Street*, published in 1946 is akin to *Native Son*. Both these writers had been preceded by the cultural movement of the 20s called the New Negro Harlem Renaissance. The Reanissance writers continually asked how a negro be portrayed in works of art. However, it was a black male-oriented aesthetic that governed the perspective of the Negro writer. Men had been the gate-keepers of Black American Literature. Even the racial struggle in the United States remained a struggle between the men of the races. Male authors portrayed male heroes and male protagonists almost exclusively. The complexity of black female experience was ignored by them. Ann Petry became the first black social realist and naturalist to depict the effects of the triple oppression of racism, capitalism and sexism on black females in the American urban ghetto environment. *The Street* forged a proletarian black women's fiction. There had been no serious treatment of black under-class women either in the narratives or early novels of the Harlem Renaissance writers. Two important elements that Petry took from Wright's proletarian protest novel were: the impact of the hostile urban environment on the black psyche and the inevitability of crime as the black person's only weapon of freedom from fear and oppression. Petry's novel poses the question of contemporary black literature: given the harshness of racism, capitalism and sexism, to what extent can a woman avoid violence and crime?

Lutie Johnson, the central character in *The Street* is representative of the many under-privileged black women who live in a bleak hostile environment where violence, rape and murder are the order of the day. The book contains vivid descriptions of the poverty and degradation in which the black population of the Harlem ghetto lives. In the opening pages of the novel Petry sets the tone of the book through the description of the bleak and poverty-stricken environment of the street in which Lutie Johnson comes to seek lodging for herself and her son.

Petry's description of the street and its inhabitants reminds one of Gloria Naylor's description of Brewster Place and its inhabitants in her novel *The Women of Brewster Place*. Like Brewster Place Petry's Street dominates the lives of the characters of the novel and becomes symbolic of their miserable existence.

Lutie is a good-looking brown-skinned girl who refuses to use her charms to further her interests. The prevailing image of a lower-class black woman is that she is a whore. Lutie too is coveted by both black and white men. Lutie is a single woman, a mother, attempting to create a better life for herself and her son Bob. She works as a domestic in the white Chandler family. In her urge to give herself and Bob a better life, Lutie tries to approximate their values and life-style. It is in this section that Petry examines the cultural transference that takes place in the lives of black women and, as it happens in Lutie's case, fragmentation of their families. Lutie begins to identify herself with the capitalistic values of the white American middle class. She wants all the things they possess and reads the fashionable glossies that they read. In staying away from home at the Chandlers for long, she loses her unemployed husband, Jim, to another woman. As she takes on the Chandlers' values, he feels inadequate and useless. He cannot find work like her. He has taken to drinking because he cannot countenance his wife's working outside the home. Lutie continues to work at the Chandlers although they are racist and sexist toward her.

Junto, the white owner of property and joints in the black ghetto, exploits the poverty and misery of black people. He exploits Lutie too and covets her sexually. In a similar way he controls Mrs. Hedges who runs a whore-house and lives in one of her apartments. William Jones, the superintendent of the building in which Lutie and her son live, constantly harasses her, treats her as a sex object and even attempts to rape her. Mrs. Hedges too looks at Lutie as a 'catch' for her boss Junto. 'A gook-looking girl like you should not have to worry about money,' says Mr. Crosse of the School for Singers. In fact nobody looks at Lutie as a decent person. She is a potential whore. Whether at the Chandler's home or at Mr. Crosse's singing school she receives racist and sexist treatment. Her employment prospects in both the white and black worlds are bleak. Boots Smith, the black henchman of Junto, craves Lutie, but is rebuffed by her. He lures her by offering her a singing job with a band he manages. Thus both Junto and Boots exploit and harass her because she is poor and single.

The Street also examines the plight of another under-class woman, Min, the battered woman Jones keeps and treats like a dog. Min comes to believe that in the hostile environment she has to live, 'a woman alone has no chance.' She therefore moves from man to man in her need for protection but ironically the very man she lives with, i.e., Jones, treats her in a beastly manner. Like all under-class women, she faces exploitation and oppression from all sides. She is a prisoner and a slave 'a live-in sex servicer' in Jones' apartment. Most of the men she has lived with have used and abused her and then discarded her. She feels she is 'ugly' and therefore she is bound to suffer. In characteristic fashion, Jones takes out his frustration on Min because he cannot get Lutie. One is reminded here of Celie's fate in Alice Walker's *The Color Purple*. Albert beats and brutalizes Celie, his wife, because Celie is not Shug, the attractive woman. Men seem to oppress women for standard reasons. After his failure to rape Lutie, Jones becomes savagely brutal. He beats Min, and hates her ugliness because he wants Lutie and cannot "get" her. In short, Min's life is representative of the lives of many women in *The Street*.

The circumstances of both Min and Lutie spring from the same social realities. Both are black, both are poor, both are single, both are victims, and both are denied employment opportunities because of their sex and color. Degraded by society and abused by men of both the races, they are nothing but sex objects. Both work as domestics for white folks who view black women as non-entities or promiscuous. Yet, Lutie does not compromise herself. From the very beginning of the novel Lutie is presented with a certain dignity and strength of character and a certain degree of self-esteem. The cold November wind blowing against her as she tries to locate the apartment building on 116th Street fails to vanquish her. Petry puts it very pointedly preparing the reader both for the environment of hostility, poverty and degradation and the valiant efforts Lutie will have to make to survive in it.

> The wind pried at the red skullcap on her head, and as though angered because it couldn't tear it loose from its firm anchorage of bobby pins, the wind blew a great cloud of dust and ashes and bits of paper into her face, her eyes, her nose. It smacked against her ears as though it were giving her a final, exasperated blow as proof of its displeasure in not being able to make her move on.
>
> Lutie braced her body against the wind's attack determined to finish thinking about the apartment before she went in to look at it.[3]

This is characteristic of Lutie for she refuses to be buffetted and blown about by the adverse circumstances which she has to continually encounter. Though she is shaken at times she refuses to be conquered. As against this Min accepts the degradation inflicted on her, because she feels an ugly, poor, coloured girl has no other choice. She has acquired what Richard Wright terms with regard to coloured people, 'dim negatives.' Min's self-esteem is very low. She has acquired a 'victim psychology,' unlike Lutie who identifies herself with the 'better class' of coloured people.

Of course, Lutie has had a better childhood. She has had a few advantages which Min has not had. Unlike Min who has been battered and sexually abused in her childhood, Lutie has not experienced any such brutality except for having a drunkard as a father, who as a man, looks upon Lutie as he would look upon any other woman. Lutie is brown-complexioned, not a 'common, nigger wench.' She could 'stick around' and has acquired a sense of 'self worth.' It is because of this that she begins to identify herself with the capitalistic values of the White American middle class. She wants her son to be educated and move up the social ladder and not end up as shoe-shine 'just like the rest of the niggers.' She refers to her husband's coloured mistress as 'that black bitch.' Yet even as she tries to approximate the values of her white employers she knows that the white racists will deny black people all that they claim and have by virtue of their birth and right. She wanted to believe that 'anybody could be rich if he wanted to and worked hard enough and figured out carefully enough.' She wants to reject the hypocrisy and degeneracy of the Chandlers but she also wants the things they possess, specially money, which she feels will allow her and Bub to leave 116th Street and all it signifies and move into a more respectable street.

Though Lutie and Min share a common plight, they are not drawn together by their suffering. Lutie looks down upon women like Min who allow themselves to become targets of men's brutality, 'a drab drudge so spineless and so limp she was like a soggy dish rag.' Both Lutie and Min lead alienated lives. Both feel there ought to be someone they could talk to, someone they could ask for advice but so hostile is the environment of the Street in which they live that they fear to be rebuffed. This is in contrast to the women of Brewster Place or to the women in Alice Walker's *The Color Purple*. The female bonding or nurturing that takes place in those novels and of the novels of black women writers of the '70s and after does not take place here. Mrs. Hedges, Min and Lutie remain isolated from one another, suspecting and hating one another.

Though Lutie puts up a brave fight as a woman she has so internalized certain sexist patriarchal assumptions and attitudes that she continually blames herself for whatever happens to her and her family. She blames herself for the disintegration of her family. She feels it is because she stepped out of her house to work for many days at a stretch that her husband was driven to philandering and her son to steal. Lutie muses,

> Not good for the woman to work when she's young. Not good for the man. Obviously she had been right, for here on this street the women trudged along overburdened, overworked, their own homes neglected while they looked after someone else's while the men on the street swung along empty-handed, well dressed, and carefree. Or they lounged against the sides of the buildings, their hands in their pockets while they stared at the women who walked past, proba-

> bly deciding which woman they should select to replace the wife who was out working all day. (65)

She blames herself for all the anger and frustration she experiences. Instead of wanting to kill her husband because of whom she has suffered a lot, she wants to kill the other woman ('the black bitch') who has taken her place in her home. Min too blames Lutie of Jones' barbarity towards her because she is powerless to do anything against Jones. Lutie is driven to murder Boots because he has tricked her into his apartment where Junto too is hiding in a back-room ready to rape her. But when Junto hears Lutie's outrage he slips out, allowing Lutie to assault and kill Boots, the black man who has persistently oppressed her. Boots projects on Lutie the hurt and humiliation he has undergone in the racist-capitalist world. He hates himself also and takes out his bitterness on her by exhibiting his manhood in his attempt to rape her, by conquering and subduing her. 'She murders him in an explosion of rage without after thought.' As mentioned earlier, Ann Petry is using two elements of Black Protest writing, viz., the impact of the hostile urban environment on coloured people and the inevitability of crime as the black man's only weapon against oppression. Bigger Thomas in *Native Son* kills two women, one white and one black out of a sense of inadequacy and fear. Petry becomes the first novelist to allow a coloured woman to kill a coloured man. Petry's novel may not go beyond protest. As Hernton rightly observes, it does not offer any positive process of affirmation and liberation from oppression. But the explosion of Lutie Johnson foreshadows the need for a more positive process of black women's liberation. Such a need was supplied by the black women writers of the '70s and '80s: Gloria Naylor, Alice Walker, Toni Morrison, to name a few. These writers offer more positive alternatives like female bonding and nurturing, coming together in sisterhood and collectively encountering the three-headed monster of racism, sexism and capitalism, without committing the ultimate act that Lutie commits. The Street in which Lutie lived with Bub had become a symbol of all that she hated, racism and capitalism, which prevented her from earning enough to give herself and her son a decent life. She also hated men like Boots who despite belonging to the same race wanted to exploit her both emotionally and sexually. Boots' attempt to rape her and then compel her to sleep with Junto, in exchange for the two hundred dollars she needed to free Bub, become the catalyst to her ultimate act. All her life's pent-up anger surfaces and finds a violent outlet.

> She was striking, not at Boots Smith, but at a handy, anonymous figure—a figure which her angry resentment transformed into everything she had hated, everything she had fought against, everything that had served to frustrate her. (429)

The murder scene in the novel illustrates Petry's thesis that crime is inevitable in a hostile environment of the kind in which Lutie and Min live. If Lutie had not continued to hit Boots, he would have raped her and even killed her. Hence, the only way left to her was to kill him. Petry gives a graphic description of the scene:

> A lifetime of pent-up resentment went into the blows. Even after he lay motionless, she kept striking him, not thinking about him, not even seeing him. First she was venting her rage against the dirty, crowded street. She saw the rows of dilapidated old houses; the small dark rooms, the long steep flights of stairs; the narrow dingy hallways; the little lost girls in Mrs. Hedges' apartment; the smashed homes where the women did drudgery because their men had deserted them. She saw all of these things and struck at them.
>
> Then the limp figure on the sofa became, in turn, Jim and the slender girl she'd found him with, became the insult in the moist-eyed glances of white men on the subway; became the unconcealed hostility in the eyes of white women; became the greasy, lecherous man at the Crosse School for Singers; became the gaunt Super pulling her down, down into the basement.
>
> Finally, and the blows were heavier, faster, now, she was striking at the white world which thrust black people into a walled enclosure from which there was no escape; and at the

> turn-of-events which had forced her to leave Bub alone while she was working so that he now faced reform school, now had a police record.
>
> She saw the face and head of the man on the sofa through waves of anger in which he represented all these things and she was destroying them. (430)

Through the murder scene Petry shows the 'causal relationship between social and personal crime.' *The Street* became the first black woman's novel to ask the question: Given the harsh and hostile environment in which the innumerable Luties lived, to what extent can they control their fate? On her way to Chicago travelling on the subway, Lutie muses:

> Had she killed Boots by accident? The awful part of it was she had not even seen him when she was hitting him like that. The first blow was deliberate and provoked, but all those other blows weren't provoked. There wasn't any excuse for her. It hadn't even been self-defense. This impulse to violece had been in her for a long time, growing, feeding, until finally she had blown up in a thousand pieces. (434)

One agrees with Barbara Christian's statement: "Petry is . . . concerned with proving her thesis that no matter how conventional and no matter how American a poor person may be, she will be defeated by her environment."[4]

NOTES

1. Calvin C. Hernton, *The Sexual Mountain and Black Women Writers* (New York: Anchor Press, Doubleday, 1967), p. 3.
2. *Ibid.*, p. 38.
3. *The Street* (Cambridge, Mass.: The Riverside Press, 1946), p. 4.
4. Barbara Christian, *Black Women Novelists: The Development of a Tradition* (1892-1976) (Connecticut: Greenwood Press, 1980), p. 67.

School of Languages,
Gujarat University
Ahmedabad

Ayn Rand's Contribution to Modern American Writing

SHOBHA SHINDE

Ayn Rand is summarily dismissed by literary critics. Her fiction is claimed to be popularist; her novels are accused of being too simplistic and her philosophy is said to be too intellectual and controversial. Nearly sixty years have elapsed after the first publication of her novels and millions of their copies are still being sold all over the world. Her books have been translated into different languages. She has become a cult-figure and has left a deep mark on the minds of younger generations. In an interview in *Playboy*, Alvin Toffler described Ayn Rand as 'an intense, angry young woman of fiftyeight, indubitably, irrevocably, intransigently individual.' In 1967, there appeared an article in *Life* magazine called 'The Cult of Angry Ayn Rand' by Dora Jane Hamblin. The author drew attention to the fact that the Institute started by Ayn Rand had 3,500 students and 25,000 graduates as members. Rand had become a visiting lecturer at Columbia, Princeton and Yale. She had received a Doctor of Humane Letters from Lewis and Clark College.

The students who came to her Institute idolized her. They became participants in a marvellous intellectual adventure. She offered her followers a comprehensive and intelligible view of existence as well as a unique vision of human nature and of human relationships. She provided them with answers to some of the most important questions of life.

Ayn Rand's fame rests on her fiction. Her stage play and her two novels deserve to be counted among the landmarks of twentieth century American literature. These books have met the psychological and aesthetic needs of multitudes of people because of their energetic ideological biases. *We the Living* (1936) is autobiographical in the intellectual sense. It tells of a girl's passionate love held like a fortress against the cruelty and oppression of a totalitarian state. Through the characters of Kira, Andrei Taganov and Leo Kovalensky, Rand tells how the Collectivist ideology is detrimental to humanity's capacity for productivity and fulfilment. Mimi Gladstein places *We the Living* in a group with *One Day in the Life of Ivan Denisovich* and *Doctor Zhivago* as it depicts the day-to-day spirit-destroying activities of life in Russia.

Anthem (1938) is a parable which depicts an era when society has returned to a stage of illumination by candlelight. The story is written in the form of a journal kept by a man of the future living in a totalitarian state, a man whose name is Equality 7-2521. He is perceived as a threat to the established order. He escapes to discover self and free will. He ends his story by uttering the most sacred word to man "Ego."

Ayn Rand's most popular novel to date is *The Fountainhead* (1946). It is a picture of the fanatic hatred and denunciation unleashed by an enraged society against a great innovator. The theme is that man's ego is the fountainhead of human progress and the novel is a dramatization of the morality of individualism. The cardinal reason for the lasting appeal of *The Fountainhead* is that it is a confirmation of the spirit of youth, proclaiming man's glory and showing how much is possible. It helps to assert the conviction that joy is possible to human beings and that doom and defeat is not our inevitable fate.

Atlas Shrugged (1957) has been described by more than one critic as 'The Bible' of Rand's philosophy of 'Objectivism.' It has been called a work of science fiction, mystery story, a female fantasy novel and a theodicy of Capitalism. *Night of January 16th* (1936) is the only play of Ayn Rand, which has been filmed and adapted to the silver screen.

It was through her fiction that Ayn Rand's message and ideas were first disseminated. According to Mimi Gladstein, 'Her fiction has made her a world-class author. It is the medium through which her message is most widely and most palatably broadcast. Even those who oppose her politically and philosophically acknowledge the impact of her fiction.'[1]

Her fiction is an illustration of her most impressive literary skill, her ability to integrate theme and plot. The philosophic ideas of the characters actually motivate and explain their actions, which in turn concretize and demonstrate the philosophic point and acquire significance. The result is a seamless blend of depth and excitement, of art and entertainment. The plot of an Ayn Rand novel is a purposeful progression of events which add upto a general thematic idea implicit in and conveyed by the story. Scientific precision is integrated with extravagant drama, vivid imagery and passionate evaluation. There is a pervasive emotional quality in her writing. The Ayn Rand characters, plot and style have become internationally known. The hero is the man of independence, of purpose, of intransigent integrity, the plot is a brilliantly ingenious structure of unexpected yet ruthlessly logical events and the style is a union of luminous clarity, intellectual rigour and passionate beauty. The indigenous combination of these is possible only to a great artist who is also a philosopher.

In the *Mirror*, Ruth Alexander wrote, 'Ayn Rand is destined to rank in history as the outstanding novelist and profound philosopher of the 20th Century.' It was because of the persuasion of her fan, Nathaniel Branden, that Ayn Rand turned to the field of Philosophy. Rand called her Philosophy 'Objectivism—a philosophy for living on earth.' The term comes from what she considered the central theme of thought that universal concepts or ideas have an objective reality. The Objectivist ethics holds man's life as the standard of value—and his own life as the ethical purpose of every individual man. The three cardinal values of the Objectivist ethics—as professed by Ayn Rand in her books and lectures—are Reason, Purpose, Self-Esteem with their corresponding virtues Rationality, Productiveness and Pride. Productive work is the central value that integrates and determines all his other values. Reason is the source, the precondition of his productive work, pride is the result. Rationality is man's basic virtue. It means one's acceptance of the responsibility of forming one's own judgement and living by the work of one's own mind (Virtue of Independence). It means that one must never sacrifice one's convictions to the opinions and wishes of others (Virtue of

Integrity). One must never seek or grant the unearned, the undeserved, neither in matter or spirit (Virtue of Justice).

Productive work is the road to man's unlimited achievement and calls upon the highest attributes of his character—his creative ability, his ambitiousness, his self-assertiveness, his refusal to bear uncontested disasters, his dedication to the goal of reshaping the earth in the image of his values.

The basic social principle of the Objectivist ethic is that 'Man must live for his own sake.' To live for oneself means that the achievement of his own happiness is man's highest purpose. Happiness is that State of Consciousness which proceeds from the achievement of one's values. Ayn Rand states that to hold one's life as one's ultimate value and one's own happiness as one's highest purpose are two aspects of the same achievement.

The Objectivist ethics proudly advocates and upholds rational selfishness. Man is objectively egoistic because truth and value, while absolute and equally applicable to all, are always experienced privately. Altruism serves as an ideal which guarantees failure as a guide for effective behaviour. It creates a chronic sense of frustration which leads to a sense of demoralization. Altruism destroys self-respect, leads to conformity, suggestibility and self-hate. The end-product is a world of muted hostility.

Rand blasted Collectivism as a Philosophy that makes man both a ward and a servant of society. It makes, in Rand's memorable phrase, 'my brother's misfortune my mortgage.' (V, 80-81) Above all, as she made clear in *Anthem*, it forbids men to use "I" and demands the use and even the worship of "We." (114) For these reasons, Collectivism is the root of war, racism, slavery and evil. She never missed a fictional opportunity to voice her indignation against Collectivism.

Capitalism, according to Ayn Rand, is the creation and in turn the creator of individualism. It is the only perfect social and economic system under which an individualist can and will thrive. The future of a country depends upon persevering the Capitalist spirit and practice.

To arrive at the conclusion of Ayn Rand's contribution to American fiction and philosophy, it is necessary to look at her life and try to discover from what experiences she has developed her vision of life.

A highly individualistic and intelligent young girl, she rebelled against the coercion and Collectivism practised in the totalitarian state of Russia. She migrated to the land of dreams, free enterprise and hopes, with her ideals. Her impressionable mind adopted itself to this new world. But she was aware that the world was slowly tilting towards the Collective will and socialism. The fundamentals of altruism, selflessness, religion and mysticism were gaining ground. Heroism, individuality, rationality and love for one's work were assuming a secondary place in the society around her. She took upon herself the challenge of issuing a warning against the dangers lurking in the dark corners of the world. At the beginning of her career she achieved her mission through her fiction. Disappointed and frustrated by the lack of intellectual recognition and encouraged by her fans, she approached the field of philosophy.

Ayn Rand never cared for cheap popularity, and the sales of her books and the name on the best-seller list never appealed to her. Her frustration resulted from the silence and listlessness of the intelligentsia who refused to take her seriously. Her scope of writing was limited, but it was deliberately so, because of the strength of her convictions. Those critics who accuse her of voicing platitudes have not understood the depth of her commitment to her cause. Her novels could be termed as 'propaganda' but they take rank and deserve a place in the annals of literature for the uniqueness of her belief.

Ayn Rand was dismayed by the fact that the Romantic Movement had died in modern times. She believed that if there was to be a Romantic Revival in the future, she would be a bridge towards it. She was firm in her belief that Romanticism was a movement that could give the world a grand new era of progress, teaching individualism and moral values. It could provide Capitalism with the philosophical aesthetic foundation for even greater achievement in future. She believed that she alone among modern writers followed the Romantic conviction that while history describes things as they are, fiction must describe them as they might and ought to be. Rand hated the idea that the essence of life is frustration, futility and tragedy. Enemies of Romanticism she felt called romantic novels 'thrillers' and branded them as 'simplistic, unrealist and escapist.' She firmly believed that literature is 'the indispensable medium for the communication of a moral ideal.' (*Romantic Manifesto*, p. 162) It was the voice of the artist's sense of life.

Her Philosophy of Objectivism provided her followers with an anchor to restore their faith in life. She called on all Americans to relearn individualism, admiration for productivity, rational self-interest and the true American sense of life. She warned them to put altruism in its place, by striking at its twin roots of irrationalism and mysticism, before it destroyed the land of the free.

Ayn Rand will always remain a popular writer and philosopher. She will be remembered as a woman who invaded that last virtually exclusive masculine domain of philosophy. She will be remembered as a novelist who was not satisfied to let her fiction speak for itself and spent a quarter of a century explaining it. She was a woman philosopher who refused to conform to any established school of thought, who insisted on nonconformity in an age of conformity. These are the things that made her unique and will make her immortal. She was the Russian immigrant girl who rose to national and international fame as a defender of American values and sense of life.

NOTE

1. Mimi Gladstein, *The Ayn Rand Companion* (Westport, Connecticut: Greenwood Press, 1984), p. 21.

Jai Hind College
Dhule

Quest for Self in the Novels of Norman Mailer

ANJOO JAIN

It has been a stark fact of nature as well as of history that man has failed to achieve unlimited freedom. This failure leads to frustration so that man begins to think that he is pitted against a hostile environment in which he is an alienated soul. This feeling has been aggravated in modern times because of social, political and economic organisations that have become so unwieldy that the sense of choice and pride of any achievement has been reduced to nullity. As such, the conflict between the requirements of the self and the demands of society has become a central issue of our time. 'Self' is the meaningful interaction of man in a given social set-up and the resultant image of his personality in that set-up. In relation to the American social set-up, the image that comes before is one that smacks of the nasty situation where disharmony, violence and several such things hold the reins of routine life and hamper the development of human personality and obstruct the path of advancement for the better future of humanity. Under such conditions, how is man to know who he is today? By what does he identify himself? This is the problem to which various American writers have put forward their arguments, seeking solution in their own way. Norman Mailer (b.1923) has rendered this theme of quest for self with more energy of style, more ideational power and more vivid drama than any other American writer to emerge since World War II.

The concept of 'self' in Mailer's novels opens out with confronting a stage of bewilderment with all the accepted values of life and suffocating institutions, leading an individual to defy all the social norms by taking risks and pushing himself to the limit of experience. This eventually leads him to self-evaluation and self-realization, resulting in the evolvement of a new, authentic way of living by confronting the very society that produces inauthenticity and crisis of identity. As such, the process of quest for self involves five well-defined stages: (a) The Bewildered Self (b) The Cultured Savage (c) The Confrontation (d) The Existential Self (e) The Crystallized Self: Perception.

(A) The Bewildered Self

Mailer in the very first stage of depicting the process of search for identity debunks the modern American society for creating a sense of uprootedness and lostness in man. He sees society as an epitome of evil which has invaded every aspect of human life. The individual is not even free to take the most private decision of his life, such as childbirth. The sexual center of the body is so deadened by contraceptives and pills that we no longer can afford to be as selective as we used to be. Hence the most natural activity has been reduced to the level of utter artificiality. All the natural chords are gradually being sapped. A man cannot find his identity anywhere. Nor in family—for that institution is breaking down. The sudden equality of the sexes creates tension in both men and women as they realize that their old roles are destroyed, but they are uncertain what their new roles should be. The big Government is the biggest enemy of the people. Mailer admits:

> the shits are killing us, even as they kill themselves . . . each day a few more lies eat into the seed with which we are born, little institutional lies. . . . Little lies but they pipe us towards insanity as they starve our sense of the real.

American society is filled with dead air which is sapping the creative energy of the individual. In an interview with Paul Carroll, Mailer argued: "the technological society sits upon us like an incubus . . . it gets between us and existence, in everything we do, the air we breath, the buildings we live in with abstract, monotonous forms, the synthetic fibres we wear."[2] The net result of this modern malady, which is often connected with "the plague"[3] by Mailer, is the dissociation between self and the physical environment, which leads to the bewilderment of the individual who is at a loss to understand his true leaning and bearings.

(B) The Cultured Savage

The second stage in the development of self implies a hard blow on hypocritical surface of society and its rotten morality by meeting them head-on, by taking risks and pushing ourselves to the limits of experience. As such, Mailer advocates the need for an intellectual attuned to his non-rational being, a 'Cultured Savage' who lives on the plane of the barbarian, giving free reins to his instincts. He warns: "What is at stake in the twentieth century is . . . peril that they will extinguish the animal in us."(*ADV*, 200) Mailer refuses to sacrifice instincts and sub-conscious needs to a civilization which is itself so little removed from savagery. Hence, he advocates free love, free sex and gives unchartered freedom to his characters in the matter of sex, love and woman. Mailer's idea of realization of the true potentialities of self is thus inextricably linked with his ideas of violence and sex. Society pressurises the self into degeneration through regimentation, mass-media and censorship, which are the subtler forms of violence. Individual violence gives one courage and hence violence is primary for the freedom of self. Mailer's idea of sexuality is strongly connected to his idea of creativity. The rebel dares to break through the armour of sexual inhibitions which eliminates one's sense of guilt. This sense of guilt is important, for Mailer, because it is the "existential edge of sex"[4] and stands as a challenge to the individual courage. If successful, the new rebel will strive to use his victory to promote personal and human growth. But at this second stage, he is little unaware of this private moral responsibility, which he gradually realizes during his quest for self.

(C) The Confrontation

The third stage in the search for identity represents a confrontation of socio-political and personal styles of identity with vitality, of the existentially naked with the imaginatively dead. It underlines the fact that concept of identity is a product of the dialectical inter-relationship between man's psyche and society, between his inner drives and external compulsions. Man's quest for identity becomes meaningful only when he realizes the integrity and inviolability of the community and is able to have a grip on the forces of life. In the search for identity, the nakeds are those who come face to face with the conditional, fragile, moral nature of his own mind and his own body, a point where props and assurances, the style of his normal-at-homeness with himself no longer avails to mask himself from himself. And if he is naked at that moment, he is also more startlingly alive than at any other moment of his life. To be naked, then is to be at once frightened, exalted and intimate with one's own most intensely conscious self. And to be dead, then truly dead is never to have such a moment, never to have watched the crumbling of the intricate style of assurances and then be forced to recognize what, amid the rubble of that fallen temple of normality, there is to assist in the construction of new and stronger selfhood. These decisive moments of judging present, the present of the naked moment admit the possibility of the past only as a preparation for it and the possibility of future only as the infinite repetition of its hieratic form. If the man's past has been one of tiny evasions, small hypocrisies, then the moment will not endure, nor will it issue, as it should, in the embracing and heroic style of being in the world. This bold search for identity definitely needs courage—the courage to face the consequences of one's action. This courage is definitely an improvement over the courage of the second stage. In the later case, anyone can have the courage to violate social taboos but this courage will endure and spring forth only in case of those who dare to face the outcome of their action.

(D) The Existential Self

The fourth stage of quest for self relates to the result and effect of individual's confrontation with his own personal void through the agency of destructive socio-political institutions or mysterious forces of Nature. The net result is that the individual perceives himself as he is, not as he imagines himself to be under the facade of optimistic illusions and euphemisms. The individual at this stage realizes that he is not a free chooser, monarch of all he surveys, but benighted creature sunk in reality whose nature he is constantly and overwhelmingly tempted to deform by his own choice of fantasy. And this realization breeds in him a feeling of despair, dread or despondency. It is at this juncture that the quest for identity takes an existential turn. One thing must be emphasized here that this feeling of dread is different from the feeling of bewilderment of the first stage. In the later case it is the result of encounter between the private self and the public self whereas in the former case, it is the outcome of encounter between private self and unmasked inner self. The feeling that he is not free even to choose (which produces Dread) is the result of the intimation of Death. Death is inevitable; this realization inspires a disproportionate terror, a horror not merely because he is going to die, but to the contrary because he is going to die badly. At each moment, he is making his way along the sharp edge of possible annihilation—this aggravated his existential anxiety.

(E) The Crystallized Self

The final stage encompasses the surmounting and conquest of barriers of dread, despair and alienation by struggling most heroically against these forces. For this, Mailer shows the path of Neo-primitivism, a belief that modern man should return to more simplified and more natural existence. Mailer does not advocate the cultivation of cultural values like love, goodwill, faith, charity etc. but contends that the only value which matters is the value which answers one's own psychological needs. And herein comes his doctrine of Hipster. Hipster believes in what Reich calls one's orgastic potencies. Mailer writes in *The White Negro*: "Orgasm is his therapy—he knows at the seed of his being that orgasm opens his possibilities and bad orgasm imprisons him." (*ADV*, 279) In other words, orgasm is a means that opens man's existential possibilities for exalted selfhood. To attain selfhood is to become a "sexual outlaw," (*ADV*, 273) to live out one's instincts:

> to be with it is to have grace, to be closer to the secrets of that inner unconscious life which will nourish you if you can hear it, for you are then nearer to God which every hipster

> believes is located in the senses of his body, that trapped, mutilated, nonetheless megalomaniacal God who is it, who is energy, life, sex, force, the Yoga's prana, the Reichain's Orgone, Lawrence's Blood, Hemingway's Good, the Shavian lifeforce. (*ADV*, 359)

Only sexual intimacy can transcend the limit of social morality and attain the cosmic harmony, but this happens only in the intimacy of "sensuous sex": "The dialogue of such sex is tender, it is respectable—it respects the slow conversion of character into mood, it seeks for an artful loss of each separate identity in order to find and give life to the 'mood' which passes from body to body."[5] The life of the body passing into 'mood' relates sex to time and eternity. Thus, there is always an element of adventure and quest in that the ultimate, the true energy is just beyond every second effort.

This pentagonal pattern comes to be the weft of Mailer's novels. His novels present the socio-political maladjustments and characters trapped in it. The series of novel appear to be a chain in which different characters pursue the path of finding the true potentialities of self and they are successful or failures depending on the authenticity of their rebellious action. *The Naked and the Dead* (1948) is an experience of the agony of American troops in the pacific campaign on the mythical island of Anopopei. *Barbary Shore* (1951) is a nympholeptic experience intended as an allegory of anticommunism which hints as well as comments on the neuroticism of postwar America. Through his *The Deer Park* (1957) Mailer wants to study debauched life where one tries to find meaning in cynical ways. *An American Dream* (1965) has a concern not with sex and death with apocalyptic treatment but with evil undisguised as war or power morality. *Why Are We in Vietnam?* (1967) is a novel with civilian protest against the Vietnam war, a symbol of collective violence. *The Armies of the Night* (1968) is a detailed account of his own part in historic Washington Peace Demonstration. Through all his novels, Mailer has tried to show that self starts disintegrating when it is beset with odd situations of combat. It loses its significance which can be restored only by heroically facing the naked moments of truth.

In *The Naked and the Dead*, different characters strive to find their true, hidden identity in the context of war situation. Some remain bewildered even after the demonic rebellion as they fail to harness their energy to face the quintessential moment. Red Valsen, Julio Martinez, Joey Goldstein, Roth and Sergeant Brown are the characters who either succumb to the fear of the ladder-structured society or fail to endure the moment of risk, panic and nakedness. Another seeker after true self is General Cummings who yearns for omnipotence: "Man's deepest urge is Omnipotence? Yes . . . to achieve God."[6] The strategy he evolves for realization of his deepest urge is to create fear in the mind of his subordinates. Cummings proves this when he forces Hearn to pick up the cigarette which Hearn leaves on the General's tent floor. He here appears to be a Cultured Savage bent on violence and inflicting atrocities on others for his own personal gains. But his triumph over others is a sour triumph since he is forced not to live through a moment of nakedness but precisely to miss such a moment when the bovine Major Dalleson gets the credit for victory over Japanese, on a day Cummings is away. Lieutenant Hearn resists the pressures for identifying himself with the power holding structure longer than any other character; but in the positive stage of transformational process, he finds that opportunity to control others satisfied a deeply felt need. Hearn's conflict with Cummings over the General's order to pick up a cigarette butt initiates the negative portion. He discovers that he is "basically like Cummings." But Hearn does not have the will-power, ruthlessness and stark confidence in his own actions as Cummings has. Hence he dies a premature death in his quest for individuation. Hearn's death comes from his decision to corporate with the system, not from indomitable rebellion against it. Hearn himself at one point remarks, "the only thing that had been important was to let no one in any ultimate issue ever violate your identity."(326) He is true neither to his inner self and its needs nor to his professed aim. Croft is the only character who faces the naked moment and endures it meaningfully. Croft has manipulated the death of Hearn so that he can assume the command and order the platoon to climb Mt. Anaka: "the mountain tormented him, beckoned him, held an answer to something he wanted. It was so pure, so austere." (497) But he fails to climb the unclimbable mountain and as he leaves the shore of Anopopei "Croft kept looking at the mountain. He had lost it, had missed some tantalizing revelation of himself. Of himself and much more. Of life, Everything." (552) But "deep inside himself, Croft was relieved that he had not been able to climb the mountain," and he is at last temporarily rested "by the unadmitted knowledge that he had found a limit to his hunger." (701) Both unexpected reactions emerge into greater clarity in the light of the more hopeful context of a man freeing himself from constraints in order to participate in a self-defining existential test. Thus the novel presents different characters enmeshed in war, trying to come out of it in their own way. Their visions get expanded but never attain to the stage of completion. Till they achieve that stage, "Only connect,"[7] Forster advised, the beast and the seer in man.

The action of *Barbary Shore* takes place around 1950 in a dingy, run-down rooming house on the cliffs of Brooklyn Heights that overlook the East River. This is Mailer's Barbary Shore, to which Lovett has come to write a novel and seeks the opportunity to live. Mikey Lovett, the protagonist/narrator, is a man without any past; he is an amnesia victim, a product of the war who is thrust with no emotional connection whatever into a nightmarish postwar world. The entire novel appears to be his attempt to come to grips with the reality—the encroaching totalitarian menace and to carve out some meaningful niche for himself. Lovett gives himself fully to the present and gets involved with the people in the apartment house. These involvements mark the progress in the search for his self. The first of these relationships begins with Mrs. Guinevere and the experience teaches him to be direct and frank about his loyalties if he is to grow in any meaningful way. McLeod, Lovett's next acquaintance, is perhaps the most important character in the novel. McLeod's rapid rise in power which is paralleled by a progressive dehumanization, an increasing commitment to expedience at the expense of betrayal and assassination gives way to sins of commission: the physical murder, first of an idealistic young subordinate and then of a personal friend who becomes unable to accept the method of the party. The degree of ruthlessness increases with his own disillusionment with Communist Policy and its culmination is reached in McLeod's role in the murder of Trotsky. McLeod did what he thought to be right at every juncture of his life and has the courage to confess it and face the consequences. As a result, he emerges wiser from his past and thinks of the broader issues than only about himself. This is reflected in McLeod's action of passing the 'little object' to Lovett and also the moral mission that goes with it. The moral mission is the establishment of a new, just society apart from Western Capitalism and Eastern Communism. Lovett accepts the moral responsibility: "So the heritage passed on to me, poor hope, and the little object as well, and I went out into the world."[8] Lovett, alone, friendless, without history, is indeed a poor hope for the future. But there is at least the hope that Lovett, after suffering all the mental dilemma and atrocities of system, will pursue his path on the basis of his own understanding of the situation and another opportunity will arise for the evolvement of a new society. Thus, to the extent that McLeod and Lovett commit themselves to future of humanity, they are the existentialists who must continually create themselves through action.

In *The Deer Park* Mailer explores more fully the psychological aspects of human experience, the need for an intense exploration of the self. And this goal is achieved through three alternative paths to the quest: the path of love and sex, the path of the rebellious artist, and the path of hipster. The keystone of each alternative is rebellion, which is the foundation of creative growth, as Mailer himself maintains, "the instict of rebellion," is the "foundation of man's consciousness, the source of his humanity and the vehicle of his evolution." (*ADV*, 233-69) *The Deer Park* is a movie colony outside Hollywood whose name, Desert D'Or suggests its desolation and artificiality. All its residents are enigmos who try to escape from their alienation through love, sex or art. To live in the real world, a world of suffering, required the courage to confront reality daily and to make the continual choice of growth over stagnation. Sergius O'Shaugnessy is rootless and sexually impotent. And he commits himself to a greater and more shameful impotence in his glee at sleeping with a universally desired woman, Lulu Meyers. The first inkling of strength in him is seen when he turns down the movie offer of 20,000. But the crisis has not yet been reached. It is only when he loses his money and Lulu and is confronted by two powerfully built insulting Government agents, because of his friendship with black-listed Eitel, that a real crisis of identity comes. But very boldly he faces the agents, fighting his own paralyzing fear. At this juncture, he attempts to plumb his own depths: "For I touched the bottom myself, there was a bottom that time."[9] Though Sergius has been able to reject the false love of Lulu, the false profession of movie star, the false values of tinsel society, he has yet not found a positive commitment. He has tried to write but is not yet able to do so successfully. Thus in this novel the artist and the art become the 'little object' in which men must rest their hopes. Both O'Shaugnessy's desire to be a writer and Mailer's glorification of art in this novel are prompted by the recognition that art can express that marriage of opposites which is so evident in actual nature of things. This dance of opposites necessitates growth. Through the story of Charles Eitel, (Pronounced "eye-Tell") and Elena Esposito, Mailer explores the way of the lover and the artist. Eitel's story, most simply put, is about a man whose ideals and actions are antithetical. By refusing to tell his leftist associations before a congressional committee investigating communists, thereby sacrificing his fabulously successful career as a movie director, Eitel affirms spirit of genuine courage and rebellion. In this case, it is rebellion against those forces in American Government that would homogenize individuals into a collective, deadening image of itself. Eitel's commercial failure gives him his new opportunity to grow. Drinking, squandering his days alone, Eitel futilely clings to his hope of writing a brave and original script. Eitel fails because the temptation of the dead, unreal world prove too much for him; his inner impulses are more in time with the world than with his ideals. After much anguish, he yields to his desire for money and status by popularizing his most recent moviescript and by co-operating with the congressional investigating committee. He is caught in a dilemma: being a hero means giving up his dream of being an artist and also means thinking of himself as a failure; being a coward means exactly the same thing. The only difference is that the former makes his position more perilous. This, of course is the way to growth but Eitel is ironically caught up in middle age. Finally he succumbs to "the sad frustration of his new middle age" (374) and tries to maintain what he has rather than risk it to grow into something new. Eitel is failure in love too. As long as he continues to discover himself over to her love, Eitel grows. But the growth is short-lived. He is frightened of her animal spirit and her appetite for experience. This unsteady foundation of need and fear poorly supports love and finally he separates himself from Elena, thus killing not only life in himself but also denying Elena a most valuable opportunity to grow. Marion Faye represents Mailer's exploration into a third way of regeneration in a dead world—the way of the Hipster. Faye is Mailer's first fictional embodiment of the hipster. The hipster, like the hipster's defiance is physically destructive, not merely destroying ideas, concepts and perceptions but destroying the actual embodiments of falsehood, oppression, homogenity. He stays close to violence, admires killing people, refuses to help friends and prompts Elena to kill herself. For Faye, there is no morality, because the conventions of society are superseded by the individual's need to cultivate feelings. Displaying no consciousness of social conditions, Faye is perhaps the culmination of Mailer's search for a self that can withstand all social exigencies and yet experience the most intense feelings. But in the intensity of feelings, Marion becomes too isolated from others and fails to grow. Marion is never able to transcend the pressure of his feelings, which drive him to a consuming self-hatred and contempt for others. As such, in *The Deer Park* characters rebel to find their identity by pushing themselves to the limit of experience but their journey is only half-way.

An American Dream explores in morbid and salacious detail, the possibilities, not for damnation, but for salvation to be found in some of the most reprehensible acts known to our society—murder, suicide, incest, fornication and physical violence. It "dramatises the various ways a man may sin in order to attain to God, become holy as well as whole by resorting to primitive psychic circuits that enable him to live in harmony with himself and find his courage, regardless of whether his courage seeks its test in the challenges of love or the temptation to murder."[10] The novel charts out its hero's exemplary struggle toward spiritual health. Rojack's involvement with murder, sodomy, fornication and other forms of physical violence is the necessary prelude to his "psychic redemption,"[11] for Mailer believes that only in successfully engaging our hidden outlaw selves can we revitalize our existence and the American myth, "that each of us was born to be free to wander, to have a venture, and to grow on the waves of the violent, the perfumed and the unexpected."[12] The way in which Rojack achieves salvation is through a courage which is constantly tested, one which is nurtured further by each successively more difficult victory. The early confrontations are faced with considerable weakness and trepidation and barely won. All of them are faced unwillingly and that is why they fail to help him in evolving any new, meaningful life style. But toward the last, there is presented a growing sense of strength and of commitment of good, as the need for evil is supplanted by something stronger and positive in nature. He realizes his true self and moves towards authenticity:

> The logic in searching for extreme situations, in searching for one's authenticity, is that one burns out the filament of old dull habit and turns the conscious mind back upon its natural subservience to instinct.[13]

After undergoing war experiences, Rojack's grace is shattered and he lives henceforth in dread, hanging over the abyss of death. He wishes to be free from these feelings and stands upon the balcony and almost jumps believing that he stands to lose his body but gain his soul. He wavers and thus his act of self-preservation proves a failure. He begins to die a little, and he feels the first flushes of cancer, that mad riot of cells, which Mailer believes is sublimated natural self-violence, consequent to the denied growth of the soul. But the drive to return to roots need not involve suicide. Authenticity results from the experience of dread and overcoming it. After the suicidal impulse on the balcony, Rojack meets his separated wife, Deborah and murders her, ostensibly as an act of internal liberation: "Marriage, to her was the armature of my ego, remove the armature, and I might topple like clay."[14] He has the courage to remove this armature, and is rewarded not by his disintegration but by the rediscovery and repression of his own violent soul. Since murder violates the most basic mandates and taboos of society, it requires an extraodinary commitment. Murder necessitates the individual's dependence upon himself and his resources and pits the individual against the society which he has rejected and which will certainly punish him for his rebelliousness if it can. And Rojack now has to face the police. He is pushed to such physical and psychological extremity during the police interrogation that he begins to feel intimations of his coming transformation if he can hold out, and the sign actually appears in form of Cherry. The union between Rojack and Cherry is a crucial test of Rojack's ability to defy chaos and stasis to create life rather than make death. In the creation of new life, Rojack must continually choose, have courage and sense of true love. In order to love, one must choose; hence love is another paradigmatic existential situation. Rojack tests his new powers and courage against the ex-prize fighter Romeo and the mafioso Tony to win Cherry from them. With each of his successes, Cherry draws closer and closer to him. But their first touch is merely sensual and they pass the deadness within them back and forth. Significantly, the turning point comes only when they turn to sex as creation. They are prepared for love:

> "Do you want her?" It asked "Do you really want her, do you want to know something about love at first?" and I desired something I had never known before, and answered: "Yes," I said, "Of course I do, I want love." (51)

Rojack is faced by the possibility of love for the first time. With Cherry, he can let himself go, surrender his self, in the sense not of a mastery—submission, as was always the case with Deborah, but of a mutual surrender in which all defenses are let down and the two can exist together in bliss. To do so required courage to face the moment of choice because the choice is irrevocable and will change his life in significant ways. In addition, his lack of defenses represents a danger for what if Cherry does not likewise surrender? But Rojack faces his dread and takes the leap into love: "now I understand that love was not a gift but a vow . . . one could find it anywhere. It was just that you could never keep it. Not unless you are ready to die for it." (123) Now onwards Rojack will have to face the worst in himself to face the disease around him. Hence Rojack's confrontation with Kelly, Deborah's father, is the climactic one. Kelly has the power to manipulate the processes of human life, of civilization, and of nature to slake his own greed, a power that by its very nature denies the enlargement of soul. When Rojack realizes the incest between Kelly and Deborah, he is compelled to face that death, that disease, which has threatened to engulf him since the start of the novel. He feels compelled to face death by a walk around the parapet. Kelly says he was never able to try the parapet, and Deborah got off mid way. Rojack must walk the parapet in order to prevent himself from dying and to protect the lives of Cherry and Shago. He walks the parapet but fails to return for a second trip for Cherry and Shago. And Cherry is killed in revenge by mistaken friend of Shago. What this means most fully requires to understand the meaning of Rojack's quest. His symbolic act of walking the parapet is essential for others as well. He has delivered himself from Satan, from the devouring maw of death and from dread but his deliverance is incomplete. Cherry's death means Rojack has not yet reached the point where he can save others by bringing his own salvation into the world. His salvation is only partial and he must continually search for life and growth in this phenomenal world.

Why Are We in Vietnam? like the novels that preceded it, is concerned with modern life on both the individual and social levels. Ostensibly, the novel consists of the narrator D.J.'s remembrance of a hunting expedition in Alaska with his father, Rusty, two of his father's business underlings, Pete and Bill, and D.J.'s best friend Tex Hyde. Below the ostensible action, however, is a complicated tale of a young man's journey into self. D.J.'s journey illustrates that despite the hero's successive acts of regeneration, he can be defeated, forced either to follow the same old path of submitting to the systems or to purge the new path evolved during the acts of regeneration. D.J.'s initiation consists of a set of voyages, deeper and deeper into the primitive Alaskan heartland, America's last frontier, and further and further into the primitive recesses of his own consciousness and the savage dreamlife of the American Continent. In so doing, he leaves behind society, civilized world, friends and parents, so that he is without external guidance and even at times without reference. The result of this hermetic experience which roughly corresponds to the second stage of Cultured Savage is heightening. Sealed off from his daily life, he finds his perceptions and insights heightened beyond what could normally be expected from him and this corresponds to the stage of 'Confrontation.' This heightening makes the character wise and heroic, at least as long as he remains in his hermetic environment. This limitation shows that man, basically having his own weaknesses, cannot reach the stage of fuller perception—'Crystallized Self,' though he makes a leap toward it. In the novel, D.J.'s father, Rusty is a quintessential distillation of the corporate spirit. Rusty's intense desire is a bastardization of the natural urge to test oneself against the force of the world, to build the self by engaging and even defeating the world outside the self. Rusty and D.J. set off alone to find a bear, and at the end of the hunt, Rusty claims their bagged grizzly as his own trophy whereas D.J. deserves the actual credit for the kill. But Rusty lies and betrays his son's confidence and his own hope for redemption. His cowardice and greed have doomed him to a frustrated, inauthentic existence. The frustration, at the sexual sphere, completely destroys Rusty's chances for psychic redemption. His wife, Hallie is a woman with love of filth, uses sex for profit and degradation. Through adroit use of threats to his masculinity, and by making him a cuckold, she has struck at the weakest part of Rusty, his deep sense of sexual inadequacy. This sexual frustration leads him to apathy and apathy leads men to surrender control over their lives and embrace the totalitarian horrors and inauthentic existence, which Rusty is leading. D.J. and Tex want to get rid of the "general state of mixed shit"[15] and undertake safari to Alaskan wilderness. They must purge themselves of the extraneous elements that have crept into their natures during the years—the neuroses of their parents, the absurd demands of their society and the corrupting influences of their peers. The two boys are observers of one natural phenomenon after another. It is on the beginning of the hunt, when Tex shoots a wolf and he and D.J. drink its blood, that D.J. realizes he is "up tight with the essential animal insanity of things." (70) The primitive, animal nature of things is both insane and forceful; it cannot be categorised rationally, operates under its own impulses, which cannot be organized into laws, and has its own intrinsic force as its justification."[16] D.J. feels the wolf's blood begin to rise inside him. Later, D.J. kills a bear and becomes an integral part of the natural order of things. His reversion to the primitive within himself is revealed most clearly when, near the close of the novel—he and Tex fare into the wilderness unarmed and encounter a wolf. The force that emanates from the wolf and from the boys engage each other in a mad, violent ballet and wolf slinks off in defeat. This is D.J.'s discovery in the wilderness that one of the great truths of existence is that every human being has at the core insanity and force of the primitive wild. Watching these manifestations of the natural world, they face dread which results from living close to death. By airing the worst in themselves, they try to overcome it and have some revelation. D.J. now hovers on the brink of discovery: "and D.J. could have wept for a secret was near, some mystery in the secret of things—why does odor die last and by another route." (196) In this novel the imagery of odor is often associated with discovering the secrets of life and creation, which is important for a fuller understanding of one's inner self. Because smell is such a direct sense, involving the actual incorporation of that which is experienced, it has been suppressed and ignored as sexuality has been limited. Mailer's wide use of the imagery of odor is, therefore, an attempt to escape from what he regards as the repressed and unhealthy state of modern civilization. Smells are key to the eternal mysteries, primarily those of conception, life and death—a key to attain to crystallized self, the last and final stage of realization of one's true self. That is why D.J. grapples with odor when he finds himself confronting the wild and the wilderness of his own nature. Thus, in a way, he is initiated into the mysteries of human experience and it appears he will complete his journey into his inner self. But he fails. After returning from his hermetic environment, D.J. has no choice but to revert to his previous decadence. He accepts the corporate competition and the war in Vietnam. This acceptance, he knows, will suffocate him but he does not have courage to rebel against society. This shows that his quest is incomplete. In this context, the novel cannot have a close end because the quests always have archetypal and cultural implications and no cultural situation can tolerate a close end.

The Armies of the Night: History as a Novel, The Novel as History is a personalized history of Mailer's own participation in the Oct. 1967 anti-Vietnam War March on the Pentagon. The emergence of this non-fictional novel is the result of Mailer's realization at the time that mass media surrounding the March on the Pentagon is creating a force of inaccurate and misleading facts. He felt that under such circumstances the alternative left open to an artist is to go back to the inner reality and to project psyche as a fictional character scrutinizing all details and facts in a lens-grinding light. Mailer explains his method:

> The novel must replace history at precisely that point where experience is sufficiently emotional, spiritual, psychical, moral, existentialist, or supernatural to expose the fact that the historian in pursuing the experience would be obliged to quit the clearly demarcated limit of historic inquiry. (284)

Here Mailer is at once denying an intrinsic and comprehensible order to history and prescribing the only possible method of understanding it, one that involves exploration of self. Mailer is aware that concentration on himself in the first section of the book has its dangers. "To write an intimate history of an event which places its focus on a central figure who is not central to the event, is to inspire immediate question about the competence of the historian or indeed, his honourable motive." (53) But he offers two justifications for his stratagem of writing about himself and suggests a third. The first and most obvious reason is that Mailer in the excess and vagaries of his character is a microcosm for America. In many ways, his personal crises and conflicts mirror on an individual scale the agonies of the American nation.

"The March on the Pentagon was an ambiguous event"(53) which can perhaps be understood only by focussing on an individual who is "ambiguous in his own proportions."(53) Second, Mailer believes himself to be at once, involved and objective; thus well fitted to the role of a historian. He only suggests the third and most important reason for placing himself at the centre of history. He realizes that it is impossible for him, or anyone else to understand any historical event, such as the March, without first understanding himself. For the modern artist, this means that the discovery and creation of his own identity is the precondition to any future endeavour; indeed one might say that exploration of the self becomes the major concern of all artistic creation. In order to understand *The Armies of the Night*, we must understand that Mailer's pre-occupation with himself is the central theme of the book. The novel is an attempt to understand, define and come to grips with his self, to describe his own human condition. His understanding of history is through the precondition of truths he learns about his own identity. In *The Armies of the Night*, Mailer very effectively brings out the disease of America, its oncoming totalitarianism, its oppressiveness and its smog. The war in Vietnam brought in open air the disease, he has written so much about; and once again while describing the long day of March on the Pentagon, Mailer epitomizes the fact that modern society is insane and schizophrenic:

> He had come to decide that the centre of America might be insane. The country had been living with controlled even fiercely controlled schizophrenia which had been deepening with years. . . . Everyday the average American drove himself further into schizophrenia. (188-89)

This insanity is the result of the split between the individual and society, his desires and the destructiveness of social institutions. Mailer records his constant premonition that "the two halves of America were not coming together, and when they failed to touch all of history might be lost in the divide."(157-58) Though he had always believed that struggle between opposing forces is the condition of existence, he had also affirmed a need for synthesis between opposing forces to resolve, if only temporarily, the struggle at the core of all existence. What he is claiming here is that in contemporary America there seems little possibility of synthesis and that the dynamics of dialectical process have deteriorated into unresolved antitheses. To fight out all the cancerous encroachments of American society on individual psyche, Mailer propounds that the beast must come forth and "grapple with the world." (36) This element of bestiality is at the centre of his and every civilized man's nature. "Mailer had come to recognise over the years, the modest everyday fellow of his daily round was servant to a wild man in himself." (13) Mailer brings forth the animality in him by his actions and the language he uses in the drunken speech from the stage of Ambassador Theatre. He was acting as the master of ceremonies and before going to the stage, he goes to men's room. It was pitch dark and he missed the bowl and soggily realized that his error would have to be confessed to the audience. He confesses it and then obscenities start coming furiously and easily: "This dwarf alterego has been telling you about his imbroglio with the P*sarrarooney upon the top floor, and will all the reporters please note that I did not talk about defecation commonly known as sheeee—it . . . but to the contrary speak of you—rye—nation." (50) We find that Mailer has succeeded in bringing the beast in himself out. And this courage gets tested in increasing confrontations. One such situation occurs after his flamboyant performance on Thursday night when he meets the disapproving stare of Robert Lowell. Mailer, the narrator, here develops the contrast of authentic and inauthentic heroism:

> You, Lowell, beloved poet of man, what do you know of the dirt and dark deliveries of the necessary? . . . the only subject we share, you and I, is that species of perception which shows that if we are not loyal to our unendurable and most exigent inner light, then some day we may burn. (54)

Lowell represents suicidal direction of American life and the impotence of tradition. And to Mailer, he is ineffective in bringing about change. Another contrast has been made between Marchers and Mailer, the protagonist. As man after man stepped forward to make his symbolic gesture against the war by presenting his draft card for burning, Mailer felt threatened by the pitiful inadequacy of such gestures. This victimization means becoming a plaything in the hands of authoritarian society and such victimization does not lead to martyrdom. To achieve the status of a martyr means deliberately doing things to offend the despotic authorities. For this reason, Mailer forces a policeman to arrest him for crossing a police line. This encounter with police helps Mailer in acquiring mighty proportions: "He felt . . . as if he were a solid embodiment of bone, muscle, flesh and vested substance, rather than the heart, mind, and sentiment to be a man." (157) The most important confrontation that gives an existential turn to Mailer's thought takes place in jail. He plans to fast throughout his term in jail. And yet before the thought has settled he takes a drink of water. He seems to himself either a saint or debauchee. The saint begins to hand out the money to pay the prisoners' fines, but the debauchee holds back the money from those he does not like. Mailer lost in these binary oppositions at last finds a way. Perhaps one ascends the moral ladder not rung by rung equivalent to each action, but by an accumulation of private acts which outweigh the negative. Though this process of exploration never attains to the stage of completion, there has always been presence of element of growth in all his novels. Here in *The Armies*, the protagonist undergoes a rite of passage, eventually synthesizing in himself not only violence but the cultural values like love and goodwill:

> The sense of the danger to the front, sense of danger to the rear—he was in fact in love with himself for having less fear than he had thought he might have—he knew suddenly then he had less fear now than when he was a young man, in some part of himself at least, he had grown. (113)

Mailer's transcendence of his condition of alienation and his movement from alienation to coherence, offers a real hope that his way of existential self-assertion may ultimately lead others to a personal integration of their fractured psyches. The March on the Pentagon is, he feels, a turning point, rite of passage. It is a possible first stirring of a new society. But this hope coexists with despair. The final passage, which conjoins images of combat, passage and birth, is as ambiguous as he believes the American situation to be. Nevertheless, the metaphor concludes with a recognition of impending birth and this in terms of Mailer's philosophy of self and its growth is ground for hope:

> Brood on that country who expresses our will. She is America, once a beauty of magnificence unparalleled, now a beauty with a leprous skin. She is heavy with child . . . she will probably give birth . . . the most fearsome totalitarianism the world has ever known? or can she . . . deliver a babe of a new world brave and tender, artful and wild? Deliver us from our curse. For we must end on the road to that mystery where courage, death and the dream of love give promise of sleep. (228)

Having struggled for fifteen years to keep alive a hope of man by keeping alive the possibility to be a man (for this, after all, was the function of his glorification of the primitive and the bestial qualities in the protagonist), Mailer well recognizes the opportunity to shift the emphasis in writing. Now he feels, the authentic man, can emerge from the night into which he disappeared and work for revolution. The March on the Pentagon is a potential turning point and moment of growth in life of an individual and society.

What makes Mailer and his philosophy of quest for self convincing and impressive is the fact that there exists in him, more so than in the case of any living American writer, a symbiotic relationship between life and art. He tries to validate the ideas advanced in his books by eventfully acting them out in the world. "Till people see where their ideas lead, they know nothing,"[17] he has said. By involving himself in the major crisis of our time—the crisis of identity—Mailer has endeavored to reanimate for Modern Man a belief in the struggle between God and Devil. Man's courage—or lack of it—against the cancerous encroachments and mass value will contribute to the outcome of that struggle. Mailer's engagements in national events represent his attempts to oppose such encroachments.

NOTES

1. Norman Mailer, *Advertisements for Myself* (New York: Putnam, 1959), p. 17. Hereafter referred as *ADV*.
2. Norman Mailer, "Vices: An Interview with Paul Carroll, from *Playboy*," *Pontifications*, p. 42.
3. *Ibid.*, p. 43.
4. Norman Mailer, *The Armies of the Night* (New York: New American Library, 1968), p. 24.
5. Norman Mailer, *Cannibals and Christians* (New York: Dial Press, 1966), p. 257.
6. Norman Mailer, *The Naked and the Dead* (New York: Rinehart, 1948), p. 323.
7. E.M. Forster, "What I Believe," *E.M. Forster: Selected Writings*, ed. C.B. Parker (London: Heinemann, 1968), p. 34.
8. Norman Mailer, *Barbary Shore* (New York: Rinehart, 1951), p. 223.
9. Norman Mailer, *The Deer Park* (New York: Putman's, 1955), p. 326.
10. John W. Aldridge, "The Big Come-back of Norman Mailer," *Life* (March 19, 1965), p. 12.
11. *Loc. cit.*
12. Norman Mailer, *The Presidential Papers*, p. 39.
13. *Ibid.*, p. 198.
14. Norman Mailer, *An American Dream* (New York: Dial, 1965), p. 27.
15. Norman Mailer, *Why Are We in Vietnam?* (New York: G.P. Putnams, 1967), p. 175.
16. Roger Ramsey, "Current and Recurrent: The Vietnam Novel," *Modern Fiction Studies*, 17 (1971), pp. 415-31, suggests that Konard Lorenz, Robert Ardrey and other contemporary cultural anthropologists are the source of Mailer's belief that violence is a necessary aspect of human and natural life.
17. Joe Flaherty, *Managing Mailer* (New York: Coward McCann, 1970), p. 118.

"It's A(n) (Un)Wise Child": Knowledge and Wisdom in the Fiction of J.D. Salinger

SUBHASH CHANDRA

The protagonists of the Glass fiction of J.D.Salinger seem to suffer from some esoteric malady, common to all of them, which turns them into tortured individuals, with warped personalities and schizoid psyches, alternating between self-flagellation and flaying others. So intense is the impact of this malady that Seymour is driven to death (he commits suicide), Buddy becomes sick of society and lives as an ascetic recluse in an "unelectrified house," Zooey, an actor, turns into a sneering cynic, nurturing a death-wish, and Franny's nerves are frayed to such an extent that she suffers from a nervous breakdown.

Various interpretations have been advanced by critics as to the genesis of the Glasses' predicament. William Wiegand, for example, maintains that "Seymour, a Bananafish himself, has become so glutted with sensation that he cannot swim out into society again. It is his own banana fever, not his wife who is at fault, or his mother-in-law" (1958:11). This delineation of Seymour does not accord with his personality as it emerges in different stories. James Lundquist, on the other hand, opines that "his [Seymour's] suicide is symbolically related to *nirvana*, the goal of Buddhism" (1976:86). But *nirvana* is not extinction. Talking about the Salinger protagonists in general, Paul Levine holds that the Salinger hero compromises the principle of "social responsibility" by choosing the "private world" over the "public world" (society) to which he refuses to adjust (1961:112).

This observation contains only half truth, since the Glass protagonists unmistakably rue their inability to relate to other people. One has therefore, to look elsewhere for the cause that drives Seymour to death and becomes the bane of Buddy, Zooey and Franny.

It is the contention of this study that the clue to their predicament lies in "It's A Wise Child"—a network radio programme, a children's quiz show. The Glasses were precocious as children and "all seven of the children had managed to answer over the air a prodigious number of alternately deadly-bookish and deadly-cute questions—sent in by listeners—with a freshness, and aplomb, that was considered unique in commercial radio" (Salinger: 1946a:48). There were times when two of them were together on the air, for instance, Seymour Buddy, and Zooey and Franny. The consensus among the listeners even after many years since the last Glass child was on the air, was that the eldest, Seymour, had been the "best" to hear, the most consistently "rewarding" and after him, in order of appeal, it was the youngest, Zooey. Franny was not far behind in coming out with most engaging answers. She once told the announcer that she was able to fly all around the apartment when she was four and no one was home. When the literal-minded announcer suggested that she *dreamt* she was able to fly, she stood her ground and said she *knew* she was able to fly because when she came down she always had dust on her fingers from touching the light bulbs. Another time the announcer initiated a discussion on housing development and the "Little Burke girl" (in Seymour's words) said "she hated houses that all looked alike." Zooey regarded them as "nice." "He said it would be very nice to come and be in the wrong house. To eat dinner with the wrong people by mistake, sleep in the wrong bed by mistake, and kiss everybody goodbye in the morning thinking they were your own family" (Salinger:1946b:54).

I would like to suggest that Salinger wants "It's A Wise Child" radio programme to be taken ironically. The Glass protagonists grow up to be voracious knowledge-hunters: they aggrandize knowledge of religions, literature and philosophy; in fact, they acquire too much of it, and in the process something happens to them, something—apart from the hostility of Matron-of-Honour ("that was the one programme on the air I always loathed," she says) and her ilk which can perhaps be dismissed as jealousy-ridden and, therefore, inconsequential—which makes them incapable of "relating to other people." With their heightened awareness, they become disillusioned with the spurious sages, ham scholars, fake-show-offs, egoistic aggrandisers and shallow intellectuals.

The very knowledge which won them acclaim and admirers through "It's A Wise Child," turns into an Albatross around their necks, and marks them out for suffering and even anguished death. No doubt, Seymour feels revolted at the over-fed, sunburned, insensitive Americans, wallowing in creature comforts and doomed to die (like the Bananafish) culturally ignorant and deprived of finger things of life, but essentially it is his disgust with himself which is responsible for his death. A discriminating heart himself, he valorizes Muriel's "undiscriminating heart," but cannot help throwing at her R.H. Blythe's definition of sentimentality, when she finds the kitten in the movie (they had gone to see together) "nice" and loveable. Muriel agrees with him that she is being sentimental, but expectedly, his "knowledge" is not very welcome, because for *living* the life, it is not "knowledge" that is essentially needed; it is the primordial, instinctive harmony with nature that acts as the sustaining force. It saddens Seymour that he should act as a kill-joy for the innocent Muriel, but it appears, he is unable to guard against using the weapon of "knowledge"; the weapon gets used by itself, against his better judgment, as it were, to destroy Muriel's radiant, naive, cheerful exuberance. He agrees with Dr. Sims that he has got some kind of a "perfection complex," and though he realises the value of living the imperfect life, accepting one's own and others' weaknesses, he finds it impossible to change. In fact, the twin factors of his disapproval of the commonplaceness, vulgarity and emptiness all around and his consciousness of causing pain to the innocent (which makes him feel disgusted with himself, as mentioned earlier) drive him to suicide.

Zooey, an actor by profession, declares: "I could happily lie down and die sometimes." Excessive knowledge has turned him into an inveterate cynic who cannot sit down to lunch, and hold his "end of a decent conversation." He rues his incapacity to do so and laments, "I either get so bored or so goddam preachy that if the son of a bitch had any sense, he'd break his chair over my head" (Salinger:1964a:85). He is cynical about Lane Coutell's motives in showing concern for Franny; he is sore at his producers, Dick Hess and Le Sage, Pomeroy and all the bunch, for being show-off mediocrities who produce third-rate, cheap, maudlin stuff and attempt to pass if off as intellectual, artistic *chef de'oeuvres*. He too, like Seymour, is aware of the negative, destructive role he inevitably plays in people's lives. Answering Franny why he would like to go to France for the movie in which he is going to act as the hero, he pours out his confession:

> I go mostly because I'm tired as hell of getting up furious in the morning and going to bed furious at night. I *go* because I sit in judgment on every poor, ulcerous bastard I know. Which in itself doesn't bother me too much. At least, I judge straight from the colon when I judge, and I know that I'll pay like hell for any judgment I mete out, sooner or later, one way or another. *That* doesn't bother me too much. But there's something I do to people's morale downtown that I can't stand to watch longer. I can tell you *exactly* what I do. I make everybody feel that he doesn't really want to do any good work but that he just wants to get work done that will be thought good by everyone he knows—the critics, the sponsors, the public, even his children's schoolteacher. That is what I do. That's the worst I do (*Ibidem*: 109-10).

One discerns, in the case of Zooey, too, a compulsive force which makes him act the way he does, and he candidly confesses that the fault actually lies with him—"It's us." He tells Franny that he is a freak, that she is a freak (though the symptoms in her case are a little delayed). He holds Seymour and Buddy responsible for their becoming freaks: "Those two bastards got us nice and early and made us into freaks with freakish standards, that is all. We're the Tatooed Lady; and we are never going to have a moment's peace the rest of our lives" (*Ibidem*:111). He and Franny disdainfully dismiss all that does not match up to their high intellectual standards, tearing to pieces everybody and everything that, to their highly charged intellects, smacks even remotely of egoism or exhibitionism.

Buddy Glass is sick of his job, sick of the society and lives, not only emotionally alienated, but also physically estranged from society without a telephone, to protect his privacy. The long letter he writes to Zooey clearly reveals his profound contempt for the theatre, Hollywood cinema, and the crass superficiality of people, self-distrust and self-castigation. He remains a recluse, with as little contact with humanity as is absolutely necessary for his physical survival.

The nervous breakdown of Franny has been seen in the Freudian light by Daniel Seitzman who concludes that Franny's sexual problem, her love-hate reaction to Lane and to other men is reflective of her religious straits (1965:57-76). In emulating the pilgrim in *The Way of a Pilgrim*, by repeating the Jesus Prayer, Franny is pursuing a spiritual ideal identified with her saintly brother, Seymour, and his teachings. But Seymour, the older brother, has also been a father figure and continues after his death as an Oedipal image for her. To love another man is for her then to deny her love for Seymour: and to deny Seymour emotionally is to deny him intellectually and spiritually as well. Thus, according to Seitzman, although she is attracted erotically to Lane, her feelings are rendered ambivalent by her effort to realise Seymour's religious goals. Max F. Schulz sees Franny's travail as religious and regards the psycho-sexual joust between her and Lane at the restaurant as "expected condiment" to introduce romantic complication in the boy-girl situation (1969:199). Franny fails to achieve what the Pilgrim could and hence her nervous collapse. "Not only is the pilgrim's way unavailable to all men, but external circumstances affect the distance he may travel down the road," says Schulz (*Ibidem*). But Franny's nervous breakdown is a direct consequence of her beginning to penetrate the layers of hypocrisy, pseudo-intellectualism, perverted values, pervading ego. She begins to hate everything, everybody and finally hates herself for doing so. She finds the humans, struggling with their total might to excel in some field and attain their ambition, pettily acquisitive and smugly egoistic which nauseates her and she withdraws from this race of midgets. In spite of herself, she spoils her date with Lane Coutell, and because she does it, she is in a nervous shambles at the prospect of the vast, arid desert which she must traverse should she not be able to restore the rapport with the commonplace, ordinary, egoistic and even mean world represented by Lane. She raves against the phoney faculty of her college, rants against the show-off fellow artists in the play she is supposed to act in at her college, and condemns outright anybody who "wants to get somewhere." The little green book, *The Way of a Pilgrim* (the sequel to which is *The Pilgrim Continues His Way*) she carries about with her (and to which Seymour had perhaps turned in his despair and depression) is not able to save her from the nervous breakdown.

The reason why the two little religious books could not save Seymour and could not really help Franny in her predicament, is ironically provided by Franny herself: "Sometimes I think that *knowledge*—when it's knowledge for knowledge's sake, anyway—is the worst of all. The least excusable, certainly. . . . I don't think it would have all got me quite so down if just once in a while—just *once* in a while—there was at least some polite little per*functory* implication that knowledge *should* lead to *wisdom*, and that if it *doesn't*, it's just disgusting waste of time! But there never is! You never even hear any *hints* dropped on a campus that wisdom is supposed to be the *goal* of knowledge. You hardly ever hear the world 'wisdom' mentioned!" (Salinger:1964a:116)

The knowledge the Glass youths have acquired does not lead to wisdom. In fact, in Taoism (Seymour thought highly of Taoism), the very nature of *knowledge* precludes wisdom: "He who is wise is not learned," records the *Tao-Te-King* (Ballou:1940:505). Also according to the *Tao-Te-King* "Not knowing that one knows is best" (*Ibidem*:501). The trouble with the Glasses is that they very much *know* that *they* know and "have translated, as it were, their awareness of themselves as special beings into a conviction on that they alone can do justice to their search for the true way . . . the brilliantly entertaining texture of 'A Perfect Day for Bananafish,' depends on Seymour's *conscious cleverness* [italics added] as well as on his conscious suffering—even his conscious cleverness *about* the suffering of 'ordinary-looking' fish" (Kazin: 1962:48-49). The love they speak of is love for certain people only—forgiveness is for the rest. They learn to love the Fat Lady—who is Christ Himself—but their love is not the love father Zossima speaks of in *Brothers Karamazov* ("Fathers and teachers, I ponder, what is hell? I maintain it is the suffering of being unable to love.") Which is surely love for the world, for God's creation itself, for all that precedes us and supports us, that will outlast us and that alone helps. "What is ultimate in their [Glass youths'] love is the love of their own moral and intellectual excellence, of their chastity and purity in a world full of bananafish with too much food. It is the love that they have for themselves as an idea," says Kazin (*Ibidem*:51).

It is ironically significant that it is the dull, repetitive, stolid, verbose Bessie (their mother) whose lament to Zooey touches the heart of the matter: "I don't know what good it is to know so much and be smart as whips and all if it doesn't make you happy. . . . At least you all used to be so sweet and loving to each other it was a joy to see" (Salinger:1964a:95). Chuang Tze, in the Taoist scripture highlights Bessie's point: "much knowledge is a curse."

Thus, the Glass fiction contains a devastating criticism of the contemporary American society which promotes Quiz-culture and puts a high premium on awareness or knowledge, unmindful of the psychic distortions it creates, which in turn lead to disharmony, discordance and unhappiness. Through Bessie's words and through the travails the Glass protagonists suffer from, the novelist emphatically asserts that the accumulation of knowledge may, in the process, dry up the stream of simple human virtues like generosity, tolerance, empathy and affection and that knowledge, shorn of everything else, may easily turn into a weapon, clamouring to attack all that is "non-knowledge," or "less-knowledge" and eventually destroy the possessor, too.

NOTES

Ballou, Robert O. 1940. Ed. *The Bible of the World*. London: Kegan Paul, Trench Trubner.

Kazin, Alfred. 1962. "Everybody's Favorite," in Henry Anatole

Grunwald, ed. *Salinger: A Critical and Personal Portrait*. New York: Harper and Row. 43-52.

Levine, Paul. 1962. "J.D. Salinger: The Development of the Misfit Hero," in William F. Belcher and James W. Lee, ed. *J.D. Salinger and the Critics*. Belmont, California: Wadsworth. 92-99.

Lundquist, James. 1979. *J.D. Salinger*. New York: Frederic Unger.

Salinger, J.D. 1964a. *Franny and Zooey*. Harmondsworth: Penguin.

______. 1964b. *Raise High the Roof Beam, Carpenters and Seymour: an Introduction*. Harmondsworth: Penguin.

Schulz, Max F. 1969. *Radical Sophistication: Studies in Contemporary Jewish-American Novelists*. Ohio: Ohio University Press.

Seitzman, Daniel. 1965. "Salinger's 'Franny': Homoerotic Imagery." *American Imago*, 22:57-76.

Wiegand, William. 1958. "J.D. Salinger: Seventy Eight Bananas." *Chicago Review,* 11:4:6-7.

Shaheed Bhagat Singh College
University of Delhi

Feminist Contribution to American Theatre: An Indian Response

NEELIMA TALWAR

Viewing the American feminist movement from close quarters has been a rewarding experience, helping me assess the position of Indian women in a comparative framework. The modernization of Indian women has run parallel to changes American women have sought, although the movements have not touched each other substantially because of their radically different historical backgrounds. From its stirrings in Mary Wollstonecraft's manifesto titled *The Vindication of the Rights of Woman* in 1792 American feminism has certainly come of age in the 1990s. It is difficult to believe that American women won the right to vote as recently as in the 1920s. Since the 1960s American feminism has raised critical questions about the nature and scope of women's identity and social roles. In the last three decades they have intensified this quest, and built many organizational support structures for greater growth of women.

A close look at the plays of two major feminist theatre practitioners will help us understand the range and depth of issues American women have been raising since the 1970s. JoAnne Akalaitis, a New York based artist and Rachel Rosenthal a Los Angeles based artist, have explored new themes and aesthetic methods to project feminist ideology. Both of them write their own scripts and create other performance related activities such as rehearsal techniques, stage design, acting methods and direction-strategies. Two important plays of these creators show their historical moorings most clearly. JoAnne Akalaitis' *Dead End Kids: A History of Nuclear Power* (1980-81)[1] and Rachel

Rosenthal's *Pangaean Dreams: A Shamanic Journey*[2] (1990-91) are important milestones of American avant-garde. These plays combine the ideological soul of feminism with the technical inventiveness of "experimental avant-garde."[3] A brief explanation of these two aspects will enable us to understand the performance-texts better.

Throughout its history, American feminism has been preoccupied with the question of the quality of life for women and the entire human community.[4] Since the 70s this quest has overlapped with the concerns of the ecology movement. In an important study of this overlap, which has been termed eco-feminism, Carolyn Merchant has pointed out:

> Women and nature have an age-old association—an affiliation that has persisted throughout culture, language, and history. Their ancient interconnections have been dramatized by the simultaneity of two recent social movements—women's liberation, symbolized in its controversial infancy by Betty Freidan's *Feminine Mystique* (1963), and the ecology movement, which built up during the 1960s and finally captured national attention on Earth Day, 1970. Common to both is an egalitarian perspective. Women are struggling to free themselves from cultural and economic constraints that have kept them subordinate to men in American society. Environmentalists, warning us of the irreversible consequences of continuing environmental exploitation, are developing an ecological ethic emphasizing the interconnectedness between people and nature. Juxtaposing the goals of the two movements can suggest new values and social structures, based not on the domination of women and nature as resources but on the full expression of both male and female talent and on the maintenance of environmental integrity.[5]

Akalaitis and Rosenthal did not write these pieces as part of a well-defined political agenda, but were deeply influenced by the political ethos and theatre-related experimentation. Interestingly, Nature has been a prime mover in drama since the late nineteenth century. Modern, naturalistic drama has been preoccupied with Nature in all its ramifications for the individual, his/her hereditary traits, gender, and environment. The modernism of naturalists like Ibsen, Strindberg and Chekhov has been deterministic. Since the 60s, post-war or post-modern drama has retained its interest in newer definitions of Nature to try and understand human destiny better. In tune with revolutionary strides made in the perception of Nature through scientific enterprise, the post-war theatre practitioners contend with the way Nature has been probed and transformed. The work of physicists in particular has "profoundly shaken the very conceptual foundations of ordinary modes of thought."[6] Particle physics or nuclear physics has been a grand obsession with theatre practitioners leading to highly cerebral plays such as *Particle Physics*[7] by Richard Foremann, *Einstein on the Beach*[8] by Robert Wilson and John Cage in which the subject-object relationship—inspired by concepts like relativity and quantum leaps—is dramatized through surreal images and language. The list is long, it may be adequate at this point to analyse the feminist contribution in the light of the American avant-garde's general characteristics. Its dominant impulse is towards experimentation: "to venture into the unknown; to try out new things; to test hypotheses against experience."[9] Three dominant features of this movement can be summed up as follows: (i) exploration of non-Western societies and their theatre work, (ii) to see performance activity as a way of connecting with or creating a sense of community, (iii) expansion of the field of performance by including many devices from the visual media.[10] A wide range of plays have been written by experimentalists. Akalaitis and Rosenthal add to this experimentation by combining form and content which has greater universal appeal.

It is noteworthy that both the performance pieces deal with Nature-related concerns. Apart from the closeness to ecological movement, and the nature-related preoccupation of modern as well as post-modern theatre, the echoes of pre-modern drama and iconography give these productions unusual historical value. In medieval allegories like *Wyt and Science*[11] and *Nature*[12] written by men, Nature and Natural Science are presented as women. A number of anthropological insights have been offered about this symbology.[13] What is most interesting, within the scope of this paper is to understand how women express their own views of Nature. Both the artists exhibit a uniquely protective vision of Earth and Nature. Akalaitis has recreated the history of nuclear science, and Rosenthal has evoked a deeper understanding of earth-related metaphors. A detailed analysis of Akalaitis's play will give us greater insight into the way these plays have enriched American creative expression.

In *Dead End Kids* Akalaitis creates a school-science fair in which the know-how of nuclear technology is displayed. It is called Atoms for Peace Science Fair. The children who see this science fair work as a leit-motif as they are receptacles of ideas that their culture institutionalizes and they build the future on these ideas. Having established children as the main text and the sub-text Akalaitis moves on to present the history of science through "multiplex method"[14] in which many independent images work simultaneously and inter-textually. The main players of this drama are scientists, the *Dead End Kids* of the title refers to scientists and generals who have used nuclear energy for destructive purposes. The history of science is presented by placing the 16th century alchemist alongside a teacher and researcher of science: both evoke the gamut of activities the alchemists and modern scientists have participated in, fusing the two historical epochs. The alchemical ritual of certain specific gestures and chants, fuses with the modern educational situation in which science is taught in secular classrooms. As David Sterritt points out, "The playing area is littered with technological icons."[15] For example the alchemy announcer comments on the aim of alchemy as "the transmutation of the alchemist himself, and that his operations are only steps in his slow progress towards, spiritual liberation." (1.4-5) A point-of-view that Akalaitis evokes with a sardonic touch. This is followed by appearance of Madame Curie who goes to work on an experiment. A woman dressed in a baseball jacket and circle skirt observes the scene. She perhaps represents the general public. The images work simultaneously, creating a tableaux, one image contradicting or highlighting other images.

We notice that powerful images from the history of science are put together, connecting the work of modern nuclear scientists such as Madame Curie to the ritualistic chants and mudras of early alchemists. As Fuch puts it, "Akalaitis' set is backed by cabalistic emblems from Renaissance alchemy and littered with children's books."[16] The early alchemists and their secret writing starts off the tradition of written formulae, published information which is transmitted from one generation to another generation. The pre-modern and the modern are re-worked further by presenting a modern lecturer and a pre-modern magician performing tricks. These images are presented simultaneously, creating a dream-like, surreal choreography in which dream-time binds the images together, allowing the audience to go back and forth in various stages of scientific history and activity. However, one should underline the fact that the dream-like state refers to the collective cultural life, in which myth, legend, and fact appear in a kaleidoscope. One of its critics has rightly said that *Dead End Kids* "offers a history of nuclear science's subconscious."[17]

With hypnotic quality, the images are amplified. From the history of physics, the focus shifts to legend: Akalaitis chooses Gretchen, Faust and Mephistopheles of Goethe's imagination.

> Madame Curie offers a translation and commentary which is improvised. She speaks English with a Polish accent. Her comments are humorous, simple, feminine. She introduces the scene with a short summary of what has gone before, the translator's name and line number in the text. Faust is seated on a grand velvet draped throne-like chair under the gold rays. The design is modelled after Durere's painting Melancholia. Spilling from the folds of the velvet are alchemical flasks, old books, bellows, stuffed lizard, stuffed birds, a skull, and various other paraphernalia that is associated with philosophy and alchemy. When Mephistopheles appears, he does so as a six headed figure appearing out of the folds of the velvet. (1.13-14)

Like earlier "inter-cultural borrowings" such as the term *mudra* from Indian semiology, referring to a well-defined gesture, in the working of Mephistopheles too the Indian impact is noticeable. Like Ravana, Mephistopheles is a multi-headed symbol of evil. An important section of Goethe's *Faust* is recited in German and English simultaneously. Mephistopheles establishes himself as "a part of darkness" which Akalaitis had earlier referred to while mentioning the alchemist's intention of "preparing darkness."

After this exchange, Faustus and Mephistopheles debate on the possibility of signing a contract for unravelling the dark forces of Nature. Very decisively, Akalaitis shows the Faustian ambition of contemporary civilization by strong telescoping of the pre-modern and modern, of myth and reality.

> At line 1415, Madame Curie translates: "Then perhaps you and I can make a deal."
> BLACKOUT on Fausthaus.
> She continues the story, summarising and commenting to the point after Mephistopheles returns and Faust agrees to sell his soul to the Devil.
> Light on a conference table STAGE LEFT of the Fausthaus.
> Faust is seated at the table, surrounded by the Mephistopheles who are in turn a businessman, scientist, army general, marine colonel, academician, and minister.
> They are each offering him a ballpoint pen.
> MEPHISTO: *Blut ist ein ganz besondrer Saft.*
> MADAME CURIE: Blood is a very special juice.
> Faust grabs a pen, looks out, enormous chord of Berlioz music. He signs six times. Various devils congratulate each other. The actor who played the alchemist, now playing the businessman, snaps a photo of Faust. (1.15)

By surrounding Faustus with Mephistopheleses who are a businessman, a scientist, an army general, a marine colonel, an academician, and a minister, Akalaitis in one shot indicates her view that her total culture feeds on (feasts on!) Faustian obsession with power and that nuclear science is a cumulative result of centuries of ambitious probes into Nature's mysteries for greater and greater power.

In a twist, reminiscent of Samuel Beckett in *Waiting for Godot*[18] from the sublime to the ludicrous, this sequence is followed by gossip about the degenerate nature of Faustus. The image of evil as nuclear science is worked out with greater emphasis subsequently. I have mentioned earlier that each focal image is amplified in great historical detail, so that we not only get a feel of the history of nuclear science, but begin to understand Akalaitis' anti-nuclear, anti-patriarchal stand quite clearly. As the following quote suggests:

> Patriotic martial music. Slides of University of Chicago plague, members of the Manhattan Project, a group in front of the atomic bomb, Roosevelt, General Leslie Groves, Truman, Churchill and Stalin.
> MALE VOICE: (In dark; solemn, pretentious)
> 18 July 1945
> Top Secret
> Memorandum for the Secretary of War
> Subject: The test.
> Sound of mikes being tapped in dark.
> MALE VOICE: Is this mike on?
> Light on conference table. General Groves and General Farrell seated behind old fashioned table mikes. Young woman as restrained but sexy army stenographer. Seated around the UPSTAGE round table are the Mephistopheles, smoking cigars and cigarettes. Throughout the following they respond to the sexual double entendres in the general's report. (1.16)

The image of Mephistopheles and Faustus, which had been woven through Madame Curie, meanders through the army generals, culminating in Oppenheimer, waiting eagerly, for the explosion. After 'this tremendous burst of light,' Oppenheimer relaxes:

> Atomic fission could no longer be hidden in the closets of the theoretical physicists' dreams. It was almost full grown

> at birth. It was a great new force to be used for good or evil. . . . The strong, sustained awesome roar warned of doomsday and made us feel that we puny things were blasphemous to dare tamper with the forces heretofore reserved to the Almighty. (1.18-19)

Man had overreached himself, Akalaitis, in her indefatigable conviction about the need for a radical transformation of her society, goes on to link this scientific event with the utterly tragic use of this knowledge on the Japanese people, and its utterly dehumanizing impact on American children. They are recipients of an educational system which fragments the lethal knowledge of nuclear science in such a way that between its science and its humane application there seems to be no contact whatsoever. This is highlighted by juxtaposing conceptual teaching of nuclear science with its effect on human beings.

> Five slides of the burned backs of Hiroshima victims are projected on the blackboard.
> The lecturer is standing over a man lying on the table CENTER STAGE. A group in lab coats is leaning over the STAGE RIGHT end of the table. All are lit by beam from the slide projector. An operation on a little chair STAGE LEFT clicks it on and off. As the group is caught in a beam they shift positions and assume a mudra. They chew gum and sporadically look at their watches. The lecturer talks rapidly, pointing to, holding up the various parts of the body on the table. The man on the table chews gum and glances at his watch from time to time. (1.32)

This mechanical, purely technical reference to a lethal activity, generates laughter followed by disgust. The presentation of a nightclub comedian presenting a performance piece titled 'The Effects on Livestock in Event of Nuclear War' with a dead chicken, enhance the feeling of disgust with man's capacity to reduce himself to a sub-human level. But what follows is even sadder in its insidious power to prepare fresh forces of evil. Two young girls are shown memorizing scientific definitions pertaining to the nuclear bomb. The play ends with the geiger counter ticking.

> After the text starts, the young woman dressed in her First Act 1950's outfit enters from the brightly lit off stage room and crosses to the geiger counter which clicks faster and louder the closer she gets to it. She runs off. The man with camera enters from STAGE RIGHT, approaches the geiger counter and takes a picture of it. On the flash, all the stage work lights and house lights come on.
>
> The End
>
> As the audience leaves the fall out shelter tape is played. (1.46-47)

Dead End Kids is a milestone in avant-grade experimental theatre. Merle Ginsberg expresses this truth when he says in his review: "*Dead End Kids* is everything you want from theatre that you never expected to get. It's a sophisticated, imagistic work that effects mostly by force of its emotional content. Though it is highly intellectual, it's never pompous; it is radically political and very funny. Now that's incredible."[19]

Akalaitis is vociferous about the political intention of the play. In an interview given to David Sterritt of *The Christian Science Monitor,* Akalaitis emphasizes her desire to take this political play to a larger audience in order to transform them. In her words: "Theatre has enormous power because it's immediate—even as a propaganda tool, to say it bluntly. In the past, theatre has shaken people up, destroyed their security, and caused them to consider enormous moral questions. That's what the Greek plays are all about—the unspeakable, the unnameable. That's what we wanted to do: to talk about the unthinkable. And also to give people information."[20]

Dead End Kids achieves this rare feat through its innovativeness. Akalaitis expressed this idea very well when she pointed out that "Theatre must somehow be in touch with the culture, not only politically or socially but also technically or people wouldn't be able to respond to it. It'll seem like a relic."[21] Plays like *Dead End Kids* are closest to the mythic and ritualistic structures of the contemporary mind. Through the liminal zone of two significant activities, that of science and of art, they fuse the two together, thereby achieving a unique act of socialization or communitas.[22] Thematically they establish a unique intercultural dialogue between two distinctly varied 'cultural activities,' structurally the rituals of 'the two cultures' are incorporated. The rituals of ancient alchemy and magic flow effortlessly into the repetitive language of modern science such as formulae, definitions, etc. The ritual-like tendency of theatre is maintained by involving the audience in the Science-Fair right in the beginning, and by making sure that the audience would be transformed by their exposure to this exposition of the history of Western civilization. It is to Akalaitis' credit that she achieves this in a stimulating manner.

Rachel Rosenthal—another powerful artist—explores "anima" themes with unusual intensity. During her tenure in UCSB as a Regent's lecturer in April-May 1991 she performed *Pangaean Dreams*, lectured on her theatre, and conducted theatre workshops to share her vision, method and analysis with the academic community. One of the important points she raised, like JoAnne Akalaitis, was the belief that art and science have to come together. This belief stems from the desire to understand fundamental existential concerns as accurately as possible. This is a highly visible characteristic of feminist scholarship.[23]

The two plays are artistic achievements that can be understood universally because the world faces ecological, economic and human problems together. The plays evoke a number of parallels in Indian feminism and the ecology movement. Traditional Indian pantheism has found radical expression in the Chipko movement of Garhwali women, and in many other concerns of Indian environmentalism.[24] It is perhaps natural that women have emerged as leaders of environmental concerns in India, both at the level of day-to-day life and its larger manifestations in national politics, because of sharper awareness of biological concerns. The work of American feminists touches a special chord because we are all in search of issues and values for collective survival.

NOTES

1. JoAnne Akalaitis, *Dead End Kids: A History of Nuclear Power.* References are based on the pre-publication script, courtesy Art Services, New York, 1981. The play has been published subsequently by *Theatre*, Yale School of Drama, 1988-89.
2. Rachel Rosenthal, *Pangaean Dreams: A Shamanic Journey* (Unpublished manuscript, 1990). The play has been conceived, written and performed by Rosenthal.
3. Richard Schechner makes the distinction between historical avant-garde and experimental avant-garde in "The Decline and Fall of the (American) Avant-Garde," *The End of Humanism* (New York: Performing Arts Journal Publications, 1982), p. 15. According to him experimental avant-garde carries many innovations of historical avant-garde (surrealism, symbolism, expressionism, etc.) in totally new direction in advance of the mainstream.
4. Sheila Ruth, *Issues in Feminism* (Boston: Houghton Mifflin, 1980), pp. 444-45.
5. Carolyn Merchant, *The Death of Nature: Women, Ecology and the Scientific Revolution* (New York: Harper and Row, 1980), p. xv.
6. For the latest assessment see Natalie Crohn Schmitt, *Actors and Onlookers: Theatre and Twentieth Century Scientific Views of Nature* (Illinois: North Western University Press, 1990).
7. Quoted in Kate Davy, *Richard Foreman: Plays and Manifestos* (New York: New York University Press), p. 1. Also see Richard Foreman, *How I Write My (Self: Play)*, *Drama Review*, 21 (Nov. 1981), p. 21.
8. Robert Wilson and Philip Glass, *Einstein on the Beach* (New York: The Byrd Hoffman Foundation, 1976).
9. Richard Schechner, pp. 15-17. American avant-garde is labelled as experimental avant-garde. See 3 above.
10. Theodore Shank, *American Alternative Theatre* (New York: Grove Press, 1982), p. 4.
11. John Redford, 'Wyt and Science,' *Chief Pre-Shakespearean Drama: A Selection of Plays Illustrating the History of the English Drama from Its Origin Down to Shakespeare*, ed. Joseph Quincey Adams (London: George G. Harrap, 1928).
12. Henry Medwall, 'Nature,' *Recently Recovered "Lost" Tudor Plays*, ed. John S. Farmer (London: Early English Drama Society, 1907), pp. 40-132.
13. See Londa Schiebinger, 'Battles Over Scholarly Style,' in *The Mind*

Has No Sex? Women in the Origins of Modern Science (Boston: Harvard Univ. Press, 1989), pp. 119-59.

14. Multiplex method is seen as a distinctive post-modern framing device. See Schechner, p. 106.
15. David Sterritt, "The History of Nuclear Power – on the Stage?" *The Christian Science Monitor*, 3 Dec. 1980.
16. Elinor Fuchs, "Too Late for Kidding," *The Soho News*, 19 Nov. 1980.
17. Joel Schecter, "Play on Bomb Booms," *In These Times*, 17-23, Dec. 1980, p. 21.
18. Samuel Beckett, *Waiting for Godot* (London: Faber and Faber, 1956). See Lucky's speech.
19. Merle Ginsberg, 'Dead End Kids: Nukes Were Never So Much Fun,' *The Villager*, 20 Nov. 1980.
20. David Sterritt, "Here's a Jaunty stage troupe in search of big themes," *The Christian Science Monitor*, 6 Jan. 1981.
21. *Ibid*.
22. See Victor Turner's explication of liminality and communitas in *The Ritual Process: Structure and Anti-Structure* (Ithaca: Cornell Univ. Press, 1977), pp. 94-97. In an important essay, "Frame, Flow and Reflection," Turner traces liminal qualities of freedom from given social structure and communitas or reaggregation after undergoing intense separation from mundane reality, in not only theatre but in every artistic and scientific activity. See this essay in *Performance in Post-Modern Culture*, ed. Michel Benamou and Charles Caramello (Madison: Coda Press, 1977).
23. This impulse manifests itself in wide ranging areas of scholarship. The literary analysis of Kate Millett's *Sexual Politics* (New York: Ballantine Books, 1969) is comparable to Ruth Hubbard's *The Politics of Women's Biology* (New Jersey: Rutgers Univ. Press, 1990) in which male bias in biological research is scrutinized.
24. Vandana Shiva is the most forceful exponent of this interrelationship. See her *Staying Alive: Women, Ecology and Survival in India* (New Delhi: Kali for Women, 1988). For other important insights see Padma Prakash, "People's Science Movement and Women's Struggle," *Economic and Political Weekly*, Vol. XIX, No. 38 (Sept. 1984), pp. 1656-58, and Ramchandra Guha, "Prehistory of Indian Environmentalism: Intellectual Traditions," *EPW*, Vol. XXVII, Nos. 1 and 2 (Jan. 1992).

I.I.T., Bombay

Indian Freedom Struggle and the U.S. Media

GAJENDRA KUMAR

Three broad trends appear from the perusal of the American press opinion concerning the Indian nationalist struggle.

A small section of the US media, with Anglophilic proclivities, often reflected pro-British prejudice in the reportings on India. Led by *The Christian Science Reporter* and *The New York Herald Tribunes*, this section had placed heavy reliance on the 'facts' supplied by the British information service in the United States. It is noteworthy that this agency published a brochure entitled, *Fifty Facts about India*. The document was distributed on a large scale and "American newspapers found it very useful whenever they needed to write editorials on the Indian problem."[1]

This group took a serious view of the activities of the Indian nationalists in the USA. Criticism of Tarak Nath Das, a prominent nationalist, for his speech at the annual convention of the Friends of Freedom of India, is a testimony to the tainted view that such newspapers published. Das was accused of abusing the hospitality of the United States.[2]

Pro-British leaning of this section further became pronounced in its commentary on the scheme of Montford Reforms (27 August, 1917). Hailing the proposed reforms as a great step forward, *The Christian Science Monitor* observed:

> The very essence of the report as has been pointed out already many times, lies in that paragraph which declares that, 'the hope of avoiding mischief in such transitional schemes lies in facing the fact that they are temporary expedients for training purposes provided the goal is not merely kept in sight but made attainable, not by agitation but by the opera-

> tion of the machinery inherent in the scheme itself.' The report makes it abundantly clear that the progress towards self-government must be by successive steps and that is for the imperial government to decide as to the time and measure of each successive advance. (January 21, 1919)

Echoing a similar view *The Los Angeles Times* hailed the Reforms as the beginning of practical political training for the Indians. It, however, added a word of caution and suggested slowing down the pace of constitutional reforms. It observed: 'Principles of representative institutions must be gradually introduced in lands where the mass of the people fall below Western standards of civilization.' (December 29, 1919)

The provisions of the Act of 1919, by and large, failed to enthuse the people. Further, the perpetuation of the extra-ordinary powers conferred on the government during the war time period through the enactment of the Rowlatt Act, roused the ire of the whole nation. The year 1919 also witnessed the most brutal manifestation of the British power in the form of Amritsar killings. Even a staunchly pro-British daily, *The Christian Science Monitor* had to depart from its usual tone. Deploring the tragedy, it wrote:

> Let it be, at once, and gladly, admitted that General Dyer is all that his friends claim for him, a worthy soldier with over thirty years unblemished service to his credit; that he was placed in a position of extreme difficulty and that drastic action was necessary. None of these things, however, alters the fact that organised shooting at Amritsar was the expression of a policy which is utterly and entirely inadmissible. The condemnation of such a policy cannot be too definite nor too final. (July 12, 1920)

However, this censure of Gen. Dyer must be treated as purely adhoc shedding of the pro-British stance. This is why the same paper gave an outrageous impression of Gandhi and his first mass movement (non-co-operation campaign) specially when even the British could not cast 'the slightest aspersion on the high sincerity of the man.' (July 10, 1921) *The Christian Science Monitor* made the following assessment about the personality of Gandhi:

> Mr. Gandhi, in spite of all his well known qualities of statesmanship which have earned for him high regard in Great Britain as well as in India, has stood revealed more and more during the past few months as the embodiment of reaction, in the simplest meaning of that word. Mr. Gandhi sees in the ways and methods of Western Civilization, in the railways, the telegraph and the modern industrial system, nothing but the ruin of India.[3]

About the Non-cooperation movement, the paper had the following uncharitable opinion:

> The Non-co-operation movement inaugurated by Gandhi the well known Indian leader, last summer, a campaign which sought to bring the Anglo-Indian government of India to a standstill by the simple refusal of all Indians, Mohammedan or Hindu, to take part in it, has proved a failure.[4]

The biased commentary of the paper can also be gauged from its bleak appraisal of Gandhi's future moves. It wrote:

> The situation in the country, generally speaking, although difficult, is not unduly serious. Mr. Gandhi has failed, so far in practically everything he has attempted, and there is no reason to suppose that he will succeed any better in the future.[5]

After the Chauri Chaura incident and the withdrawal of the non-co-operation movement there was comparative lull on the Indian national scene. The arrival of the all-white Simon Commission revived the U.S. media interest in India. The Commission was greeted with black flag demonstrations. Wherever it went in India hostile crowds everywhere displayed placards and banners that read 'Go back, Simon', but *The Philadelphia Inquirer* had altogether different analysis to convey. It reported:

> The attempt to boycott the Commission has apparently failed and this is a sign of good omen. There are many Indians who believe that they have a better chance of justice at the hands of a British commission than at the hands of their own countrymen. If Sir John Simon and his colleagues fulfil expectations, they should be able to do a great service for India. (February 7, 1928)

The failure of the Simon Commission to mollify the national sentiment resulted in the famous Lahore resolution of 'Poorna Swaraja' (1929) and the subsequent launching of the Civil Disobedience movement by Gandhiji. In England preparation went ahead for hosting the First Round Table Conference despite the decision of the Congress to boycott it. While the majority of dailies and periodicals expressed doubts about the efficacy of the conference in the wake of the Congress boycott *The Christian Science Monitor* viewed it as a positive advantage. It wrote:

> So many influential Indians will, after all, attend the coming "round table" conference in London also to raise reasonable hopes that any agreed decisions which this gathering may reach will command sufficient support in India to enable them to be put into operation. It would, no doubt, have been well if Mahatma Gandhi and Indian Nationalist leaders had been willing to participate. There are compensating advantages, however, in the very abstention of these extremists, for this has rendered possible a wide range of representation than would otherwise have been the case. (September 13, 1930)

The same paper was critical of Gandhi and his mass campaign. In one of its observations, it accused Gandhi of letting loose lawlessness by inaugurating the Civil Disobedience campaign. It wrote:

> It is obviously not easy for any government to arrest a "saint" for collecting salt on a bleak and deserted seashore, especially when the "Saint" himself was courting arrest. On the other hand, there are objections to waiting until many innocent people have perished before arresting the instigator of lawlessness unless it was clear that to have arrested him before would have led to even greater bloodshed. But the arrest is clearly justifiable as it is, and greatly as the Mahatma himself probably welcomes it as a possible further impulse to the cause to which he had devoted himself. (May 8, 1930)

Pro-British leanings of these papers and periodicals were amply reflected in their response to the 1942 Quit India struggle. Reacting to the Congress Resolution for British withdrawal from India *The Baltimore Sun* observed that the vast majority of the American people would support the British if they took any action against the Congress: '*The Washington Star* and *The Philadelphia Inquirer* counselled the British to take the sternest measures against the Congress while *The New York Herald Tribune* grimly indicated that there was no longer any room for argument with Gandhi.'[6]

Thus, it is clear that a section of the American press sought to project an attitude of hostility while commenting on Indian nationalist activities. They almost spoke the British imperial versions on the events taking place in India. However, there were some newspapers and journals, too, which strove to maintain caution and objectivity in their coverage on India-related issues.

The New York Times was the representative daily of such publications that often took a neutral stance tinged with slight positive observations on issues concerning the national struggle. Although initially *The New York Times* had disapprovingly commented upon the activities of the Indian nationalists in the USA, it did not hesitate to revise its comment in the light of new disclosures. It wrote:

> The whole case (against Indian revolutionaries in the USA) is being tried at the instigation of the British government.

> The United States government has never found anything seditious in the writings of these defendants. (March 1, 1918)

The same paper further made a guarded observation about the Montague-Chelmsford Reforms. While it branded the Reforms as an imperfect arrangement 'as a means of educating the Indian people in self-government,' it was quick to add: 'For whatever the outcome of the Reforms recently introduced in India, they will add to the general stock of political experience.' (March 6, 1920) In the meantime events of gigantic dimensions were taking place in India but little credible news was coming forth. Hence, *The New York Times* observed:

> Little news goes out of India. The censorship is doing its work thoroughly. But occasional correspondence appears in English newspapers to yield hints of what is going on under the stricter Government policy since the arrest and imprisonment of Gandhi. (June 11, 1922)

It is noteworthy in the context of the Gandhian movement that a section of the press held Gandhi responsible for the spate of violence that followed in retaliation against the British repression of mass movement. *The New York Times* did not share this sort of appraisal. It stated: 'Mr. Gandhi makes no appeal to violence; in fact he distinctly preaches against it; but it is clear that his ideas have an explosive power and will have to be handled carefully.' (January 9, 1921)

The New York Times did some plain speaking when it editorially commented that India's demand for self-government could no longer be answered by a recital of the good works of the British Raj. It observed: 'Yet despite such reservations, the historic argument for liberty stands. If India is determined to be free, one cannot go on indefinitely pleading the benefits of British rule. Neither can one use in the old form the argument that India is not yet ready for independence.' (May 28, 1930) Thus, there did exist a section of American press which though usually responsive to the Indian aspirations of freedom viewed their struggle with some reservation but without any pronounced bias.

However, the stand of the liberal press was entirely different. It took absorbing interest on the notable happenings in India. Represented by *The Nation, The New Republic* and *The Christian Century* and many others, this group remained a consistent supporter of India's cause, from the very beginning. Particularly, after the advent of Gandhi on the national scene, this liberal section of the press threw its full weight behind the national movement in India.

Though the details of the Punjab happenings appeared quite late, the liberal press was quick to register its anguish. An article condemning the British atrocities in the Punjab, appeared in *The Political Science Quarterly* on December 20, 1920. The author observed:

> Never before, except in Ireland, has the British name been sullied by a crime so black. Other, if minor, atrocities followed elsewhere in the Punjab, where for a time ruled a reign of Terror. The Indian Government not only condoned all these atrocities, but it suppressed by every means in its power a knowledge of the facts. When against its will, the Hunter Commission, an inadequate and partial Commission, was sent out to inquire, it hastened to pass an act of indemnity to shield the perpetrators.[7]

Further, the reports of the Hunter Commission came under scathing criticism at the hand of these sections. *The Nation*, a leading periodical, criticized the report for its mild depreciation of the massacre. The journal commented:

> Of course, says the report in effect, bombing villages from airplanes sometimes results in the death of innocent persons, and this is deplorable; but in general, it is the method we feel called upon to approve. Of course, if people assembled in an illegal gathering refuse to disperse they must be fired upon, but it is worthwhile even at the expense of several seconds' time to order them to disperse before killing them. Thus have argued tyrants and their apologists in all ages. When the Czar shot down hundreds of peaceful peti-

> tioners "illegally assembled" before the Winter palace in January 1905, he doubtless argued as the Hunter Commission argues with regard to Amritsar, when the Germans dropped bombs on the British babies in English villages they doubtless urged the same necessity that forces British airmen to drop bombs on Indian babies in defenseless villages in the Punjab. The history of atrocity and the history of autocratic military rule are one and the same. And the nation which builds that sort of history, be it Russian or German or British or American, is doomed to the horror of the war with its neighbours and to rebellion at home.[8]

The British government in the meantime had sought to mollify the enraged sentiments by Montford reforms proposals. *Asia*, a notable periodical, carried out a detailed critical analysis and opined:

> Now it is certain that the proposals made by the Government are in every respect so insufficient and so disappointing that they cannot fail to produce a very bad impression—are in fact at this moment producing a bad impression throughout India.[9]

The periodical also had a dig at the professed objective of the Reforms (progressive evolution of a Responsible Government in India and its slow pace). It further observed: 'It would take two hundred years at that rate, and perhaps longer to establish for India any system of genuine self-government under British leadership.'[10]

The liberal press hailed the emergence of Gandhi and his unique method of launching anti-British campaign. His humble appearance and moralistic approach in politics greatly impressed the liberal media. His resort to fast as a means of penance for the acts of violence that marred the visit of the Prince of Wales was picked up by *The New York Times* for comment. The paper stated: 'As a remedy for the situation for which he is responsible a responsibility he has the decency to admit Gandhi has imposed upon himself a complete fast for one day each week.' (Nov. 22,

1921)

The visit of the Prince of Wales generated so much heat that the British government felt panicky and ordered large scale arrests. The arrest of the Congress leaders and other nationalist volunteers was disapproved by *The Nation*. It commented:

> With these wholesale arrests and sentences has gone no charge that the victims advocated violence. The English are taking strange methods to secure the peace of India or an enthusiastic welcome to the Prince of Wales and he, at least, ought to be a good enough sport to know it. To imprison men for peaceful non-cooperation is to invite violence. Perhaps the British raj thinks it would be easier to deal with that than with Gandhi's tactics.[11]

Gandhi continued to hit headlines in the American media ever since he launched the non-co-operation movement. In fact, it was through him that the American interest in the Indian affairs could be substantially aroused. The American journalistic community came to view him as the strongest man to lead the nationalist movement. 'A perusal of the American press with respect to the non-co-operation movement reveals frequent reference to Gandhi's personality, his life and career. His new technique of revolution was closely interwoven with the movement that the American press found it hard to dilate upon the struggle for Swaraj without making a reference to his personality and method of warfare.'[12]

Liberal papers, in fact, were flooded with articles, notes and commentaries concerning Gandhi. Writing about the charismatic personality of Gandhi, *The New York Times* observed:

> The government of India in its own country is the most powerful government in the world and has met and overcome many an obstacle in one way or another, but today it is up against an obstacle of a sort which is brand new in its experience. It is up against M.K. Gandhi, a dark little wisp of a man who looks as if he could be picked up in one's arm and carried off like a child. In point of personal following he is

> far and way the greatest man living in the world. . . . He specialises in reducing his wants. He has fasted long and so often that he physically is mere shadow of a man. He is an idea, a living force in a frail and brittle body. (July 10, 1921)

The Nation had more brilliant appraisal of Gandhi. It wrote:

> In an age men call cynical, materialistic and disillusioned the national hero and leader of India is a saint whose singular devotion, unselfishness and spiritual power have won him the almost superstitious reverence of his own people and the respect of the most sceptical critics. At a time when the Western world is unable to think of concerted resistance in other terms than those of war, Gandhi has been able to persuade the organised Indian national movement to use non-co-operation as its weapon. The freedom of India, he realizes, may have to spring from the blood of her heroes, but he pleads, 'Let it be said by coming generations that the only bloodshed was our own.'[13]

Yet another complimentary comment appeared in *The New Republic* on July 27, 1921, in which a parallel was drawn between Gandhi and Jesus. The journal commented:

> When Mr. Gandhi calls on his followers to renounce the social order which the British Raj has imposed on India, to give up titles and offices, to refrain from courts, to withdraw their children from government schools and above all to abstain from violence, "to hold every English life and the life of every officer serving the government as sacred as those of our own dear ones" he is following more closely the methods of Jesus than any leader since Saint Francis.[14]

It is to be noted that the Gandhian tools to combat the imperial menace created some misgiving in certain quarters. But *The Nation* struck a positive note when it observed:

> At least, if Gandhi succeeds in spite of all obstacles and in

> the face of growing desire of many Indians to use violence, it will mean that mankind has at last found a way to war. The peace of the world depends upon the perfection of some methods of non-violent resistance to imperialism.[15]

Next to the non-co-operation movement, the visit and subsequent reports of the Simon Commission drew the attention of the American media. The liberal periodicals and journals did not take for granted the findings of the commission as emanating from sources which could not be questioned. *The Christian Century* stated:

> The fact that the report opens with a reiteration of the same promise that was included in the Montague-Chelmsford proposals of 1919, again emphasizing the fact that the grant of self government depends upon the guarantees of maintenance of order of the import and British commercial interest in India plainly foreshadows a report so cautious and so hedged about with reservations as to fail to satisfy most considerable body of Indian opinion.[16]

Sharing the concern expressed by *The Christian Century, The Nation* too dubbed the Simon Report as utterly inadequate to meet Indian aspirations. It observed:

> It will not soothe the troubled water of India but will gravely inflame the populace. It will make impossible the proposed October Round Table Conference. We doubt if even the Indian moderates will now be lured to that proposed parley. Indeed, we believe that it puts the final seal upon the long struggle which began with Gandhi's march to make salt, and, for better or worse will not end until the Indian peoples are in complete control of their own destiny.[17]

In the meantime disillusionment of Gandhi with the British had led to the launching of the Civil Disobedience movement. One remarkable thing about this movement was that the American sympathy for the cause of India was more pronounced than that of 1921. *The Nation* was forthright in supporting the native cause of self rule. It stated:

> We cannot see how any body who believes in American institutions and the principles underlying them can hesitate. India has just as much right to take over its own government today as the Americans had in 1776. It is not for us, nor for the British either, to sit in judgement upon the fitness of these people to rule themselves or to prophecy what the future may hold in store for them.[18]

As the nationalistic upsurge began to touch new heights after the Second World War, the battle lines were finally drawn with the Congress demanding complete British withdrawal from India and the US media demanded for an American initiative to resolve the crisis. *Life* published an 'open letter' to the British people. The letter cautioned the British that the USA should not be identified as a collaborator in the perpetuation of the British rule in India. The magazine asserted that the Americans were surely not fighting the war for the preservation of the British empire elsewhere. While appreciating the British predicament in India *Life* stated, 'We do not see that your "solution" to date provides any evidence of principles of any kind. In the light of what you are doing in India how do you expect us to talk about "Principles" and look our soldiers in the eye?'[19] Further, *The New Statesman* and *The Nation* took initiative to urge President Roosevelt to act as a mediator to break the political impasse.[20]

Thus, the liberal press viewed Indian struggle with sympathy and favour. They had always an appreciative comment for our valiant struggle. Imbued with ethical standards, they believed in the inalienable right of the people to manage their own affairs.

However, the whole course of a survey of the response of the US media is plagued with two major constraints. Firstly, all was not well with regard to free flow of news from British India. The rigid British censorship often prevented those news items to make their way to the outside world which might embarrass them. The paucity of news from India did not go without notice. *The New York Times* observed:

> Little news gets out of India. The censorship is doing its work thoroughly. But occasional correspondence appears in English newspapers to yield hints of what is going on under the stricter government policy since the arrest and imprisonment of Gandhi. (June 11, 1922)

Paucity and distortions of news from India was also discussed by *The Nation*. It editorially commented: 'Once more we deplore the lack of an American news service in India. We are obliged to depend for news of tremendous import upon fragmentary and biased semi-official British dispatches.'[21] The same paper was 'sceptical of official hand-outs meant for American consumption.' It was constrained to observe, 'News is what the news agencies choose to make it particularly Indian news. We read that the Prince of Wales landed at Bombay amid a tumult of enthusiasm and that the city decked itself in gay colours to greet him. . . . Official welcomes we take for granted; of the native reception we should like to know more. Not so much the New York papers as official propaganda in India is responsible for the distorted stories that reach us. Whenever there is violence in India the authorities blame it on Gandhi. Falsely,—for to anyone who reads Indian papers it is plain that Gandhi does his uttermost to restrain violent expression of the growing bitterness against British exploitation.'[22]

In fact, as late as the 1930s the USA did not have a first-hand reporting facility from India. Thus, for want of first-hand and accurate information their comments were influenced considerably by the highly professionalized anti-India propaganda by the British in America. Propaganda on behalf of the British was kept at a high pitch. Sponsored visits by the so-called British experts on Indian matters was a notable ploy resorted to by the British to conduct its disinformation campaign. The following remark of Lawrence Frederic Rushbrook Williams, Foreign Minister of Patiala that appeared in the issue of 10th May, 1930, amply demonstrates the partisan and deliberate distortion indulged by the British:

> The outbreak (Civil Disobedience) had been sporadic and

> could not be classed as constituting a revolution throughout India, any more than a riot of students in Barcelona could be justly described as a rising against the government of Europe. . . . Gandhi reverenced by his followers as a prophet or a mystic but not as a real political leader.[23]

Nothing can be more than such a wide of the mark review of the Gandhian movement. Moreover, such an observation was not solitary in its kind. Such exaggerated and tainted analysis was often fed to the American opinion so much so that the noted novelist Pearl S. Buck had to bemoan: 'The press is so adverse to anything but the imperialistic point of view that we could scarcely hope for any publicity on any Indian discussion.'[24]

However, the American media in due course began to place lesser reliance in the news items funnelled through the British sources. After 1930, many of the media establishments began to station their own correspondents in India. Hence, the proportion of objective reporting increased in the US papers and journals. While it is true that the American Fourth Estate as a whole did not always vigorously endorse the Congress point of view, it is also noteworthy that 'they did not seek to black out news and views in favour of India. The daily press carried brief reports of meetings where freedom for India was demanded and the policies of the British were scorned. Newspapers as well as journals published several letters to the editor reflecting varying views on the Indian issue.'[25] In fact, the pro-nationalist side was never shut out from the press or the radio.

To conclude, it should be appreciated that the American newspapers and magazines provided a vital channel for nationalists by virtue of which they managed to get their communication past British censorship. Further, the news items and relevant data of press facilitated the task of airing pro-independent views by American Senators and Representatives. Press clippings were often used by pro-Indian elements in their correspondence with White House officials to draw their attention to the Indian problem. Moreover, American newspapers were often sounding boards for the Indian nationalist leaders. Last but not the least, probing and reporting of the American newspapers about the nationalists kept the issue alive and boosted their struggle. Press concern did touch the British conscience after the Second World War when the media insisted that the crusade against totalitarianism would be inconceivable without attainment of self rule by the then subject peoples of Asia.

NOTES

1. M.S. Venkatramani and B.K. Srivastava, *Quit India: The American Response to the 1942 Struggle* (New Delhi: Vikas, 1979), p. 279.
2. *The New York Times*, March 13, 1917.
3. Harnam Singh, *The Indian National Movement and the American Opinion* (New Delhi: Ramakrishna), p. 166.
4. *Ibid.*, p. 184.
5. *Ibid.*, p. 185.
6. Venkatramani and Srivastava, p. 228.
7. Bernard Houghton, 'Reforms in India,' *Political Science Quarterly*, XXXV, December 20, 1920, p. 549.
8. June 19, 1920, p. 814.
9. "Unrest in India and a Remedy," *Asia*, XIX, July 1919, p. 67.
10. *Ibid.*
11. December 21, 1921, p. 717.
12. Harnam Singh, p. 160.
13. XIII, September 14, 1921, p. 282.
14. *The New Republic*, p. 232.
15. November 10, 1921, p. 557.
16. June 18, 1930, p. 771.
17. July 1930, p. 1.
18. May 21, 1930, p. 588.
19. *Life* (Chicago), 13 (12 October 1942).
20. Venkatramani and Srivastava, p. 300.
21. November 30, 1921, p. 609.
22. *Ibid.*
23. *The New York Times*, 10 May 1930.
24. Venkatramani and Srivastava, p. 279.
25. *Ibid.*, p. 234.

R.D.S. College
Bihar University

Detente as a Device of American Dominance in the World Affairs

P.M. KAMATH

After the end of World War II, the U.S. emerged as the single most powerful nation in the world affairs. Others like France or Britain on the allied side became weaker than they were before. The defeated countries like Germany or Japan were totally vanquished. But only one country the USSR an allied power had still the capacity to challenge the American dominance of world affairs, though it was as a poor second. Even though a partner in the war efforts on the allied side, the USSR was completely unlike the Americans in their government system, political ideology, and economic organization. Hence, once the raison d'etre in marriage of convenience was withdrawn, the USSR became a natural and chosen adversary of the US.

The US assumed the role of leadership of the Western world to make it safe for democracy. In this, after considerable internal debate, the US accepted 'containment' of communism as their major foreign policy goal. Thus, the US foreign policy, since 1945, has revolved around the single most important consideration of containing the growth and expansion of the Soviet power. This naturally gave rise to the cold war between the two super powers. The cold war lasted until 1972. A new device of managing international relations—detente—was devised by Nixon when he became the President in 1969. The aim of detente was to maintain American dominance in the world affairs even in the absence of cold war. This paper proposes to discuss the use of detente as a device to maintain American dominance in the world affairs.

What is detente? Going by the dictionary meaning it refers to relaxation of international tensions. Lawrence L. Whetten gives 15 different interpretations of the term as given by different policy-makers and policy-analysts. Different governments with different perspectives at different times have given or relied upon one or the other interpretation of the term. It is not necessary here to catalogue all the interpretations given to the concept of detente. Suffice it if I state some important meanings of it. The Soviet scholars, for instance, have not accepted it as a different phase in their bilateral relations with the US. For them the term meant acceptance of peaceful coexistence by great powers as it was first propounded by Khruschev in 1954. Another more acceptable meaning of detente is involuntary convergence of interests of super powers on major contentious issues.

Detente is not the opposite of cold war, which is complete peace. But difference between the cold war and detente is crucial too. Under the cold war dominated bilateral relations, there was conflict in every field of relations resulting in complete adversary relations. But under the detente, there is cooperation in certain areas resulting in corresponding relaxation of tensions. At the same time conflict and competition continue in other areas. As Coral Bell puts it, "Cold War assumes a conscious maintenance of tensions at relatively high level. Whereas detente supposes a conscious and deliberate reduction of tensions."

Detente is necessarily an instrument of management of tensions in the world affairs. For the management to succeed, it is necessary to identify issues where cooperation could benefit more than confrontation and therefore, aim to reduce the area of disagreement. Hence, Whetten defines detente as compartmentalizing cold war into manageable framework. In the light of the above discussion, I may define detente as a policy of nations in adversary relationship to deliberately explore and expand areas of accommodation while the tensions and distrust persist in other areas.

Nixon and the First Detente

It was president Nixon who for the first time took a conscious decision to replace cold war with detente in the US relations with the Soviet Union. It is interesting to note that of all people it was Nixon who masterminded this policy. Because, his entire record as a politician since 1948, shows that he was an anti-communist crusader and a diehard cold-warrior. But from the strategic perspective, such a dramatic change in American foreign policy from cold war confrontation to limited US-Soviet cooperation in world affairs could be brought about only by a President who enjoyed impeccable credentials as an anti-communist. This is necessary in democratic politics, merely to sell the policy to the public without inviting a charge of sellout. Hence, his predecessor, Lyndon Johnson could not have implemented such a policy of relaxation of tensions.

In this sense detente was initiated and formalized by Nixon when he visited Moscow in May 1972 and signed the SALT I treaty with the leader of the Soviet Union, Brezhnev. In another sense, a slow process of detente had set in the US-Soviet relations, since the Soviet Union proclaimed adherence to the policy of peaceful co-existence in 1954. Thereafter, even when the cold war was at its height, the US and the Soviet Union took a small step of great significance when they cooperated in securing the treaty of Antarctica whereby 12 nations declared their adherence to use the icey continent for peaceful purposes without making any territorial claims.

Since then a thaw in cold war was slowly developing in their relations. It is not necessary for the purpose of this paper to go into the details of this thaw. Yet it may be mentioned here that the Cuban Missile crisis of 1962 was a major step which only further paved the way for the limited Test Ban treaty (August 1963), the White House-Kremlin Hot line (September 1963), Outer Space treaty 1966 and the NPT 1968 as other major steps before Nixon arrived in the White House in January 1969. But it must be reiterated here that when Nixon chose to follow detente as a policy there was a qualitative difference in contrast to the evolutionary steps taken by his Democratic predecessors and his own conscious policy of detente.

Rationale for the Nixonian Detente

Why did Nixon decide to follcw detente as a policy in the US relations with the Soviet Union? There were many hardpressing compulsions which motivated Nixon to embrace the policy of detente. These may be considered under different categories like military, technological, economic and political—both domestic and international.

In the area of military compulsions we must note the fact that during the decade between 1962 and 1972 the Soviet Union had made considerable advances in all fields of defence preparedness. The Cuban Missile crisis of 1962 had humiliated the Soviet psyche. The Soviet negotiator, Kuznetsov had then said: "All right Mr. McCloy, we will get the IL-28s out as we have taken the missiles out. But I want to tell you something. . . . The Soviet Union is not going to find itself in a position like this ever again." And it was at that point, that the Russians started their big surge in strategic weapons.

By the 1970s the Soviet Union had moved from the nuclear inferiority to parity according to American liberal thought and to superiority according to the conservatives. They had bridged the gap in the air force. They had no blue water navy worth the name in the 1960s but had developed naval presence in all the oceans. In this background the US policy-makers concluded that simple vertical acquisition of nuclear weapons and possession of over capability under the doctrine of mutually assured destruction (MAD) really did not help because the Soviet Union was matching the US by adding a weapon for a weapon thus leveling up to the US at a higher level.

The situation had made face to face conflict between the two super powers unthinkable. Only conflicts in which two sides tried to establish one upmanship were proxy conflicts. In these, nuclear weapons were unusable as shown by the Vietnam war. Where nuclear weapons were used as a demonstration of the US political will to act, as in the case of Bangladesh war, the Soviets too demonstrated that they too could literally follow the Americans in their game by following the US nuclear-powered Enterprise. Thus, there was a painful realization in the US that henceforth, the nuclear superiority was unattainable, thus accepting nuclear sufficiency.

The conclusion was also supported by the technological factors. Technology involved in maintaining nuclear superiority was becoming too costly and complex both on grounds of economy and technological progress. New technology that was developed to keep pace with the Soviet Union and that was needed to maintain superiority was turning outdated even before it was fully applied. Technological developments were making new strides so rapidly that political and military leaders were unable to keep pace with changes and their complexities so as to grasp their significance for political strategies to be followed in the super power relations. This compelled the policy-makers to introduce a degree of policital stability in international relations.

Not only technology and rapid changes in it had gone beyond political comprehension of policy-makers, but they had created an economic problem for the US by demanding enormous sums to be invested in the development of newer technologies. But the Americans had drained their economy through a bloody war in Vietnam since 1960 which was no way nearing the end of the tunnel. The war had created a balance of payment crisis, never seen since the end of Korean war, dollar had weakened and the other economies, particularly, like those of West Germany and Japan, were emerging as rivals to the US. During the period, the Soviet Union had not only moved ahead in military and technological area but was emerging as a competitor to the US in attracting many nonaligned countries to their side by offering them foreign aid and taking up their political causes.

There were certain political compulsions as well—both international and domestic for detente.

There were vital international political considerations. In the 1950s and to a great extent in the 1960s Western Europe had accepted the US leadership of the West in their ideological confrontation with the Soviet Union. But in the 1970s Western Europe had become uneasy at the idea of nuclear or non-nuclear confrontation of the East and the West. This uneasiness was particularly intense in the nation close to the line of confrontation i.e. West Germany. The European discomfiture is explained by their doubts as to the credibility of the US nuclear protection in the event of a military threat from the Soviet Union or Warshaw pact led by it. In the 1960s the US enjoyed military preponderance created by the nuclear superiority. The US was then perceived to be capable of retaliating the Soviet first strike, and still survive to attack. But in the 1970s as stated earlier the Soviet Union had caught up with the US in every branch of the armed forces including the nuclear strategic weapons. In such a situation, will the US risk a nuclear attack on its own territory to protect the Western European countries from a Soviet conventional attack? The West European countries were not convinced.

These doubts naturally made France to develop its own nuclear deterrence; while West Germany was willing to give up Adenaur's idea of German unification first and detente later and instead move towards establishing contacts with East Germany as a part of Willy Brandt's Ostpolitik and the unification was to come as an outcome of detente. In this background the European states were not willing to blindly accept the US leadership and confront the Soviet Union in international affairs.

There were domestic political compulsions as well. Nixon had won presidency on a strong campaign to end the Vietnam War. But the War was nowhere near the end; on the other hand he had intensified the war, extended it to Cambodia. But without ending the War, he could not dream of winning a second term. But at the same time he realized that he could not end the war without active cooperation of both the benefactor nations of North Vietnam—the Soviet Union and China. These two were also in competition to retain and maximize their hold over North Vietnam at the same time realizing that the War has been a drain on their resources too.

Thus Nixon set on a course to change the American foreign policy from cold war to detente. With a carefully crafted summit meeting held in February 1972 in Beijing, the US normalized its relations with China. This was followed by a visit to Moscow in May 1972 wherein the two leaders signed the SALT I treaty thereby formalizing detente. This is the military side of detente which tried to regulate growth of nuclear weapons instead of competitive growth.

Thus the message to North Vietnam was very clear. As Nixon

was negotiating with Brezhnev and cementing detente with a bear-hug, the US was pounding Vietnamese targets with heavy bombing. North Vietnam was not happy at the Soviet Union and China trying to be friendly with the US; but a contrary message was clearly written on the wall. This led to North Vietnam agreeing to peace terms in October 1972 which were formally signed in Paris in January 1973. Nixon's international diplomacy of detente brought him rich dividends in the grateful nation reelecting him with landslide majority in November 1972 elections.

The most important consideration for a detente in the erstwhile adversaries, however, came from a basic realization on the part of the US that its military and economic power has declined vis-a-vis the Soviet Union if not in absolute terms at least in relative terms. Hence, Nixon was keen to exploit the ideological and nationalistic differences between the Soviet Union and China which had become public by early 1969 when the two fought a border war and China declared the Soviet Union as her enemy number one.

Zbigniew Arzezinsk had spoken about two and one half balance of powers. In this equation China was half. Thus until then this half weight was deemed to be on the Soviet side by the US policy-makers like President Johnson and his Secretary of State, Dean Rusk. But now on the theory that an enemy's enemy is a friend, the US under Nixon drew China closer to the US so that the US could still maintain her dominance in world affairs.

Reagan and the Second Detente

Another Republican Ronald Reagan ran on a conservative platform in 1980 elections. In comparison to Reagan, Nixon appears to be liberal in his approach to the Soviet Union. Reagan like Nixon, however, possessed high credentials as an anti-communist. Once in the office he swiftly acted to implement his campaign promises to make the US number one military power once again. He increased the military budget, revived the B1 bomber, cruise missile and refused to hold any summit meeting with the Soviet; after all, they personified, in his opinion, an "evil Empire." His equally staunch supporters in the NSC, began to unfold plans to roll back communism in the Soviet Union. For instance Prof. Richard Pipes said in 1981 that "detente is dead" and unless the Soviet Union changed from the communist model to capitalism, war between the US and the Soviet Union was inevitable.

President Reagan's predecessor, Jimmy Carter had the agonizing experience of taking a complete turn-about from the original policy approach of continuing the detente initiated by Nixon and pursued by Ford. But the Soviet invasion of Afghanistan had forced him to revive the cold war in 1979. But Reagan had no such agonizing moments, as he had been against detente even when it was introduced by Nixon in 1972. Hence, he decided to raise the cost of Soviet presence in Afghanistan by embracing Pakistan as the frontline state to channelize military assistance to Afghan fighters.

Reagan's military pressure on the Soviet Union in Afghanistan was with a clear intention to make it their Vietnam. Well orchestrated international opposition to the Soviet invasion of Afghanistan forced the Soviet Union to seek a change in the cold war relations to a second phase of detente after the start of Reagan's second term in January 1985. With the rise of Gorbachev in the Soviet Union, President Reagan found a right kind of leader in the Soviet Union to continue his search for detente with the aim of establishing unchallenged supremacy of the US in the world affairs.

After two summit meetings in October 1985 (Vienna) October 1986 (Reykjavik) the two agreed on INF treaty which was signed at the Washington summit in December 1987. This was the formalization of detente between the two super powers.

Once again another very staunch anti-communist, Ronald Reagan became the architect of the second detente. In retrospect, his policies to some extent laid the foundation for the unprecedented act of ending the cold war along with the collapse of the Soviet Union; though it is Gorbachev who deserves most of the credit. As Joseph S. Nye, Jr. rightly said: "Reagan's military budgets, his rhetoric about strategic Defence Initiative and the INF deployment in Europe all played a role, but the primary answer to (what changed American attitude towards Cold War) is

Gorbachev."

After Gorbachev assumed power in the Soviet Union, he realized that the Soviet economy cannot go on as it was in a very bad shape. His main item on the agenda was an economic recovery, for which he rightly realized that he needed peace which he cannot achieve unless he was willing to end the cold war with the U.S. and her allies. If Gorbachev was to plagiarise parts of President Kennedy's inaugural address and deliver an address, he could have said: Let every nation know whether it wishes us well or ill, that we shall pay any price, bear any burden, meet any hardship, support any friend, oppose any foe to assure the survival of our economic reforms and march towards freedom and liberty.

That apart, there were also hard realities on the American side too. The first and the foremost was the simple fact of economic considerations. President Reagan was elected on a self contradictory programme of reducing taxes domestically and raising the defence expenditure to make the U.S. number one power in the external affairs. He had also promised to balance the budget by reducing deficits. However, Reagan realized that in spite of curtailing certain welfare programmes, he simply could not go on raising defence expenditure and holding on to the reduced tax structure for ever. The budget deficit had mounted beyond proportion—more than what he inherited from the Carter administration. This fact received a public confirmation when in October 1987 a crash in the New York Stock Exchange sent panic signals to the developed countries. This made compulsion to reduce defence expenditure more urgent.

There was also the President's concern for his own place in American history books of future. Close aides, friends and Nancy Reagan felt that the President had an image of a cold warrior and warmonger. He should leave his prints as a peace maker as well. It is remarkable for a man of Reagan's intransigence in dealing with the Soviet leaders to suddenly become impatient to achieve concrete results. This is shown by the fact that once the peace process began with the first meeting in October 1985 he met Gorbachev at five summit meetings before he left office in January 1989.

George Bush Pushes towards the End of the Cold War

President George Bush continued his push towards the stabilization of detente. He continued the trend set by Reagan in continuing the arms reduction agenda and maintaining cordial and personal rapport with Gorbachev by holding summit meetings. It is not necessary for purpose of this paper to go into the details of developments since Bush assumed Presidency. Suffice it if I state that the Gulf War created by the Iraqi invasion of Kuwait, put Gorbachev in test in maintaining detente and moving beyond, to end the cold war. In this Gorbachev completely aligned himself and the Soviet Union, with the UN (read U.S.) war aims. Since then events in the Soviet Union have moved so rapidly that as Czechoslovak President Vaclav Havel said in 1990 in his address to the US Congress: "We have literally no time even to be astonished."

But these events have brought the curtain down at least on the first act when the erstwhile Soviet Republics declared their independences one after the other and formed on December 8, 1991 a loose confederation called Commonwealth of Independent States. James Baker reacting to it said on that day: "I think the Soviet Union as we have known it no longer exists." Subsequently Gorbachev resigned and became the last President of the Soviet Union.

Since then the US has in effect become the only super power and every act seems to be going the way Americans propose. There is much to be happy about the long term policy goal of containment of communism. From now on, as President Bush said in March 1990 in his National Security Strategy report to Congress, "our goal is to move beyond containment." Towards this goal, he had sought "integration of the Soviet Union as a constructive partner in international system." President Yeltsin of Russia, the successor state to the Soviet Union, has said that Russia and the U.S. are no longer enemies.

These recent developments again show clearly that second detente initiated by Reagan and the subsequent developments have clearly established the American dominance in the world affairs.

University of Bombay

The Global Impact of America's Relative Economic Decline: Theoretical Implications

RAJESH M. BASRUR

For the past two decades or so, the global economy has been in a fluid and uncertain state. On the one hand, there has been a rapid growth in international transactions, which had led to increasing integration. On the other, there has been a simultaneous disintegrative trend in the form of growing competition among the big players and a movement toward the formation of regional economic blocs. The latter phenomenon has been widely associated with the relative decline of American hegemony in the world economy. In this brief paper, I will assess the import of these contradictory trends for neorealist systems theory and its variant in international political economy, hegemonic stability theory (HST). Strictly speaking, neither theory is directly concerned with state policy and its formulation. Nevertheless, both are relevant to policy-making because they claim to illuminate the underlying structural realities that constrain some policies and facilitate others.

Neorealist systems theory holds that, in the anarchic system of world politics, states pursue power and self-interest, and hence politics is of a competitive nature. (Waltz, 1979) A variation on this holds that the global system is generally dominated by a hegemonic power, which organises the system's activities in such a way as to ensure stability while at the same time satisfying its own interests. (Gilpin, 1981) Starting with the same basic framework of systemic anarchy, HST maintains that markets are inherently unstable and that stability can only be provided by a hegemonic power which is willing to ensure order by acting as a stabiliser.

(Mavalankar, 1986:19-45; Gilpin, 1987:72-80) A corollary to both neorealist systems theory and HST is that the decline of a hegemonic power brings instability to the system.

From the historical standpoint, the global economy has experienced two periods of hegemony: the Pax Britannica of the nineteenth century and the shorter Pax Americana of the period between 1945 and the late 1960s. Both were eras of relatively free trade and growth in the international movement of goods and money.[1] The decline of British hegemony led to the rise of competitive, nationalistic policies and the liberal trading regime collapsed with the outbreak of World War I. The inter-war period saw a similar breakdown of efforts to stabilise the system. After World War II, the US emerged as the new hegemon and once again established a relatively liberal and stable regime through fixed exchange rates and the General Agreement on Tariffs and Trade (GATT) with the objectives of promoting monetary stability and progressively reducing trade barriers.

By the late 1960s, American hegemony could no longer be sustained. The relative decline of the US occurred because of the rise of the European Community (EC) and Japan. (Mack, 1986; Bellon & Niosi, 1989:9-65) True, as some writers have observed, the US remained the leading economic power in many respects. (Strange, 1982; Russett, 1985) But by the 1980s, it was clear that it no longer enjoyed the kind of dominance it had exercised during its heyday.

The American share of world exports fell from 20% in 1957 to just over 10% in 1987. (International Monetary Fund, 1988:132-3, 144-5) During roughly the same period, the trade balance of the US shifted from a positive one of $ 4.89 billion in 1960 to a negative one of $160.28 billion in 1987. (International Monetary Fund, 1989:724-5) As late as 1981, the US had been the world's largest creditor; but by 1987, it had become the world's largest debtor, with net foreign liabilities of over $400 billion. (Aho & Levinson, 1988:22) On the technology front, the American share of global research and development expenditure, while still large, declined from 40% in 1970 to 33% in 1983. (Lalkaka, 1988:37) Similarly, the American share of world patents (a measure of innovation) fell from 24.3% in 1975 to 17.7%

in 1984. (Ibid.:38) By the late 1980s, Japan had achieved greater efficiency in product quality, labour productivity and the utilisation of state-of-the-art computerised flexible manufacturing systems, and had also cornered the world market for the latest generation of semi-conductor chips. (Ferguson, 1989)

What are the effects of this structural change from American hegemony to a multipolar distribution of economic power? Both neorealist systems theory and HST anticipate increasing instability, strains on the existing regime and its institutions, and a retreat from the integrative trend of the decades under American hegemony. Indeed, there is some evidence of this. Fixed exchange rates have long been abandoned, while the Uruguay Round of GATT negotiations has been marked by serious disagreements among the major actors, notably on the question of trade in agricultural commodities. There appears to be a trend under way toward the formation of regional "superblocs" centred on the US, Japan and the EC. (Garten, 1989) There is also some similarity to the pre-World War I and the inter-war periods in the growth of "New Protectionism" (Gilpin, 1987:204-9) or "neo-mercantilism." (Geiger, 1988) Symptomatic of this is the proliferation of non-tariff barriers to trade, such as so-called "voluntary restraints" on exports and technical specifications designed to prevent imports. By 1983, 30% of the product groups in manufactured goods consumed in the developed countries were subject to some sort of import restriction. (Gilpin, 1987:207)

The US itself has been unable to resist this trend. It now lays stress on "fair trade" rather than on "free trade." Unwilling to tolerate "free riders" any longer, and unable to bear the costs of system-maintenance by itself, it has exhibited a new determination to exert pressure on its trading partners by using its still considerable economic clout. Jagdish Bhagwati observes that the US is displaying a "diminished giant" syndrome which is "reflective of the psychological mood of a nation losing hegemony in the world economy." (1988:103) Thus, in 1986, when South Korea decided it was cheaper to buy wheat from Argentina than from the US, the US pressurised the Koreans into "voluntary import expansion." (Ibid.:105-6) Peter Evans has pointed out that, in taking retaliatory action against "unfair traders" under the 1979

Trade Act, the Reagan Administration carefully chose to exert pressure "in precisely those sectors in which the U.S. felt it had strong comparative advantage: services (Korean insurance), agricultural exports to advanced countries (Japanese tobacco and EC canned fruits), and high-technology manufactured exports to industrializing countries (Brazilian informatics)." (Evans, 1989:220)

On the other hand, American policy has not abandoned either the multilateral approach to negotiations nor the liberal economic system itself. Thus, despite its tough bilateralism on many issues, it has continued to try and achieve its objectives of institutionalising trade in agricultural products and services through GATT, thereby "riding two horses at the same time." (Bhagwati, 1988:104) The key question, therefore, is: why has the US continued to repose a basic faith in maximisation of international exchange with as few restrictions as possible?

Neither neorealist systems theory nor HST is able to provide an adequate answer. Both place too much emphasis on the role of the anarchic structure of the system, which constrains cooperation and facilitates competition when the distribution of power is multipolar. Critics of these theories have used different arguments to explain the paradox of simultaneous cooperation and conflict in the system. John Ruggie argues that the post-war global economy reflects "the compromise of embedded liberalism," which involves shared perceptions on the positive value of a liberal regime as well as the acceptance of numerous exceptions in the form of safeguards, exemptions and restrictions. (1983) In his view, the survival of the regime in spite of America's decline reflects the continuance of shared purpose. However, the argument is not very convincing because it glosses over the dichotomy of purpose, which has led to the rise of competitive unilateralism in American policy even as a significant commitment to multilateralism remains. Ruggie's case clearly understates the significance of the extent of which structural change (i.e., power distribution) has affected orientations toward the global system.[2] The problem here is analytical: Ruggie offers no theoretical basis for distinguishing between cooperation and conflict when they occur simultaneously in the system.

Duncan Snidal, in criticising HST, asserts that, despite the decline of a hegemon, regime-maintenance by a small group of states is possible. (1985) His central point is that "all states do not have to coordinate collective action as long as some effective k-group can cooperate."[3] (Ibid.:599) Snidal concludes from his analytical exercise of a three-member k-group that "the hope for the coalition [of all three] must rest with the strategic rationality of states and their realization that defection will lead to the complete collapse of cooperation." (Ibid.:610-1) Thus, his theory rests ultimately on the group members' knowledge that non-cooperation can result in regime collapse, with high costs incurred by all. He does not consider the extent of these costs, which are surely essential to any conception of strategic rationality. If the expected costs are very high, there is a strong incentive to cooperate. To come to some sort of estimate of this, it is necessary to look at the objective situation, i.e., the question of what is at stake in regime-maintenance. It is simple enough to assess this by measuring the quantum of interactions among states and estimating their value to the states. But first, it is necessary to introduce interactions conceptually into systems theory. This, as I will show, makes it possible to refine neorealist systems theory so as to enhance its explanatory power in the current context.

Neorealist systems theory, most rigorously developed by Kenneth Waltz, distinguishes between "structure" and "process" in a system. (1979) A system itself is an analytical construct, a lens through which any number of interacting units (in this case, states) may be examined. Process, which consists of specific relationships among states (e.g., arms control, trade), is not considered relevant to system-level theorising because it is determined by state-level factors, such as the role of elites and national economic needs. Structure is a property of the system alone, not of its constituent parts. Its two components are: (i) anarchy, which impels states to seek power and pursue self-interest because of the absence of a controlling sovereign; and (ii) the distribution of power, mainly among the major actors, which determines basic patterns of state behaviour that accord with different power configurations.

As I have pointed out, structural theories predict that, in an anarchic system, the shift from American hegemony to multipolarity will bring increasing competition and, correspondingly, declining collaboration. The introduction of a new variable—the intensity of interaction—helps elucidate why, in fact, a high degree of collaboration persists. Theorists who stress interdependence do say something similar, but the concept of interdependence has a primarily positive connotation, i.e., it is widely assumed that there is a parallel process of rising cooperation along with rising interdependence. My conception of interaction maintains that cooperation is necessitated only at very high levels of interaction. At lower levels, either cooperation or conflict is possible, depending on what structure induces. This explains, as I will show below, why the decline of American hegemony has not led to the kind of conflictive state behaviour that emerged in the wake of Britain's hegemonic decline. As regards the theoretical aspect, intensity of interaction (or simply, intensity) fits well into systems theory because it is a property of systems rather than of their individual members. It emanates from the members and yet stands apart from them.

The concept of intensity is not new. Ruggie brings out Durkheim's conception of "dynamic density," which refers to "the quantity, velocity and diversity of transactions that go on within society." (1986:48) Nye, in passing, mentions "the intensity of international interdependence" as a characteristic of systems. (1988:249-50) Keohane specifically refers, also in passing, to the "Intensity of interactions" in his critique of Waltz. (1986:22) None of these liberal thinkers systematically develops the concept. In my view, intensity modifies the role of structure in a system. When intensity is low, structure is of little significance. With rising intensity, the role of structure increases, resulting in either cooperation or conflict. When intensity is very high, structure recedes in salience, and, even if structure tends to induce conflict, a high degree of cooperation is evident. The changing role of intensity, and hence of structure, is briefly described below in the context of the evolving global economic system.

The emergence of today's integrated world economy is relatively recent. Walt Rostow's measurement of the index of world trade (1913=100) shows that the volume of world trade in 1750 was only 1.70. (1978:669) It was only after the mid-nineteenth century that a global system emerged with the growth of trade, an international money market, increased coincidence of business cycles, and growing similarities in price and interest rate trends. (Ashworth, 1987:72-3) Rostow's study reveals a rapid growth in trade after the middle of the twentieth century: 1913=100, 1948=103, 1958=187, 1968=407, 1971=520. (1978:669) Recent statistics show a similar trend. The total value of world trade rose from $592.2 billion in 1970 to $3, 846.2 billion in 1980, and further to $5,866.3 billion in 1989. (International Monetary Fund, 1990:120-1, 124-5) There was also an acceleration of financial flows in the 1980s. Cross-border bank deposits of nonbanks shot up from $559.6 billion in 1981 to $1,351.2 billion in 1989. (Ibid.:83) Cross-border bank credit to nonbanks (by residence of borrower) grew from $670.9 billion in 1981 to $1,389.8 billion in 1989. (Ibid:78)

Before the middle of the nineteenth century, when global transactions were insignificant (low intensity), the impact of structure was negligible. After 1850, as intensity increased, the role of structure grew. Because of its great economic strength, Britain emerged as the hub of the system, dominating trade and finance. (Ashworth, 1987:211-6) Structure facilitated first cooperation in the era of British hegemony, then conflict in the wake of Britain's hegemonic decline, and again cooperation under American hegemony after World War II. The decline of American hegemony has revived the structural tendency toward conflict, but, as the data show, the process of integration has continued.

Despite the growth of protectionist sentiment in the US, the EC and Japan, there has been no serious sign of looming trade wars and systemic disintegration. Efforts to resolve problems through concerted action have been abundant. Since 1975, the Group of Seven leading industrial countries (G-7) has held annual summits for the coordination of macroeconomic policies. GATT has not been abandoned despite much friction on the question of trade in agricultural goods. The Basel Concordat (1987) marks the beginning of a long-term effort to stabilise the global financial system. When private sector banks were seriously threatened by the debt crisis of 1982, the lending countries coordinated their strategies to enforce discipline on the banks as well as the debtor states. (Kapstein, 1989)

Thus, it is clear that, in the context of very-high-intensity interaction, structure has played a greatly reduced role in the system. Instead of straightforward disintegration and rising conflict, there is a more complex picture of both cooperation and conflict occurring simultaneously following America's relative economic decline. Admittedly, the concept of intensity is somewhat imprecise, because it is difficult to identify a threshold between one level and another.

While this problem needs to be tackled in the future, I believe the analysis as a whole stands critical scrutiny. Thus, it is possible to predict with some confidence that, despite the expectations of neorealist systems theory, the global economy will not collapse, and there will be no trade wars. Very-high-intensity interaction has established a self-sustaining cooperative system. Retreat into reduced interaction is not a viable option because it would decrease markets and efficiency, thereby bringing structural decline, which, in an anarchic system, is unwelcome from the economic as well as the military standpoint.

NOTES

1. Strictly speaking, a hegemon need not prefer a liberal system. In practice, though, such a system would be preferable because of the lower costs involved in maintaining a system which benefits many others.
2. Ruggie also ignores an alternate (and more convincing) view of the so-called postwar compromise: that it emerged as the outcome of bargaining between a hegemonic power and weak allies dependent on it for their security.
3. A k-group consists of a minimum (unspecified) number of states among whom the benefits of cooperation outweigh the costs. By definition, free riders outside the group are tolerated.

Bibliography

Aho, C. Michael & Marc Levinson (1988), *After Reagan: Confronting the Changed World Economy* (New York: Council on Foreign Relations).

Ashworth, William (1987), *A Short History of the International Economy Since 1850*, 4th ed. (New York: Longman).

Bellon, Bertrand & Jorge Niosi (1989), *The Decline of the American Economy*, transl. Robert Chodos & Ellen Garmaise (Montreal & New York: Black Rose Books).

Bhagwati, Jagdish (1988), 'The United States and Trade Policy: Reversing Gears,' *Journal of International Affairs*, vol. 42, no. 1 (Fall), pp. 403-60.

Evans, Peter B. (1989), 'Declining Hegemony and Assertive Industrialization: U.S.-Brazil Conflicts in the Computer Industry,' *International Organisation*, vol. 43, no. 2 (Spring), pp. 207-38.

Ferguson, Charles H. (1989), 'America's High Tech Decline,' *Foreign Policy*, no. 74 (Spring), pp. 123-44.

Garten, Jeffrey E. (1989), 'Trading Blocs and the Evolving World Economy,' *Current History*, vol. 88, no. 534 (January), pp. 15-6, 54-6.

Geiger, Theodore (1988), *The Future of the International System: The United States and the World Political Economy* (Boston: Unwin Hyman).

Gilpin, Robert (1981), *War and Change in World Politics* (New York: Cambridge University Press).

______ (1987), *The Political Economy of International Relations* (Princeton, NJ: Princeton University Press).

International Monetary Fund (1988), *International Financial Statistics: Supplement on Trade Statistics, 1988* (Washington, D.C.: International Monetary Fund).

______ (1989), *International Financial Statistics Yearbook, 1989* (Washington, D.C.: International Monetary Fund).

______ (1990), *International Financial Statistics Yearbook, 1990* (Washington, D.C.: International Monetary Fund).

Kapstein, Ethan B. (1989), 'Resolving the Regulators' Dilemma: International Coordination of Banking Regulation,' *International Organisation*, vol. 43, no. 2 (Spring), pp. 323-47.

Keohane, Robert O. (1986), 'Realism, Neorealism and the Study of World Politics,' in Robert O. Keohane, ed., *Neorealism and its Critics* (New York: Columbia University Press).

Lalkaka, Rustom (1988), 'Is the United States Losing Technological Influence in the Developing Countries?' *Annals of the American Academy of Political and Social Science*, vol. 500 (November), pp. 33-50.

Mack, Andrew (1986), 'The Political Economy of Global Decline: America in the 1980s,' *Australian Outlook*, vol. 40, no. 1 (April), pp. 11-20.

Mavalankar, Anand P. (1986), *International Political Economy: A Critical Introduction* (Ahmedabad: Harold Laski Institute).

Nye, Joseph S. (1988), 'Neorealism and Neoliberalism,' *World Politics*, vol. XL, no. 2 (January), pp. 235-51.

Rostow, W.W. (1978), *The World Economy: History and Prospect* (London & Basingstoke: Macmillan).

Ruggie, John Gerard (1983), 'International Regimes, Transactions and Change: Embedded Liberalism in the Postwar Economic Order,' in Stephen D. Krasner, ed., *International Regimes* (Ithaca, NY & London: Cornell University Press).

______. (1986), 'Continuity and Transformation in the World Polity: Toward a Neorealist Synthesis,' in Robert O. Keohane, ed., *Neorealism and Its Critics* (New York: Columbia University Press).

Russett, Bruce (1985), 'The Mysterious Case of Vanishing Hegemony; or, Is Mark Twain Really Dead?' *International Organisation*, vol. 39, no. 2 (Spring), pp. 207-31.

Snidal, Duncan (1985), 'The Limits of Hegemonic Stability Theory,' *International Organisation*, vol. 39, no. 4 (Spring), pp. 579-614.

Strange, Susan (1982), 'Still an Extraordinary Power: America's Role in a Global Monetary System,' in Raymond E. Lmobra & Willard E. Witte, eds., *Political Economy of International and Domestic Monetary Relations* (Ames, IO: Iowa State University Press, 1982).

Waltz, Kenneth N. (1979), *Theory of International Politics* (Reading. MA: Addison-Wesley).

Ramnarain Ruia College
Bombay

Politics of Technology Transfer: The US and India

SANDHYA SHARMA

In the recent years, the developing countries have shown increasing interest in acquiring high technology from the developed countries. The reason for this is the "transmissibility character" of modern technology that makes it advantageous for the developing countries to import technology. It is widely understood that a developing country can technologically gear up its production at a higher level through import of technology than through internal evolutionary process. Import of technology creates the possibility of "leap frogging" the technology gap. Moreover, the rise of newly-industrializing countries (NICs), which have been able to grow and export rapidly with comparatively meagre technological infrastructure, is an example of new development strategies that other developing countries would like to adopt. Clearly, there are important advantages in a country being a technology follower, commonly referred to as "advantage of latecomers."

Awareness of the role of technology in economic development has made the developing countries' voice their demand for transfer of technology from the developing countries at concessional rates. This demand of the South has moral under-currents as it requires the North to atone for the past sins of economic exploitation of the South. Reaction of the United States to this has been to reflect "sensitivity to the demands of the developing world, while continuing to maintain a position supportive of the world market system."[1]

Position of the US on technology transfer to the South is reflected in the following three approaches adopted during the 1970s.[2] First, the US proposes a basis for making available to the South high technology that were largely controlled by the North on highly concessionary terms. An example of such transfer of technology is satellite-based programmes for accumulating and disseminating informations. Secondly, the US stresses the importance of joint educational and training programmes for the South to expand the understanding of potential benefits from the application of new technologies. Thirdly, stress is laid on the importance of the private sector's role in technology transfer. It is pointed out that since most of the technology sought by the developing nations was controlled by the private sector, it is essential to create an atmosphere in which individual companies would contribute not only capital but also management, technology, and access to world markets. Such technology transfer is opposed by organised labour in the US. Moreover, the developing countries have resorted to several changes in the mode of technology import like, replacement of direct investment by transfer of technology to non-affiliated firms, lower royalty fees, and an end to confidentiality requirements. These changes are resisted by American businessmen. Such domestic constraints delimit the US government's capacity to use technology as an instrument for foreign policy.

Yet, there is a will to use technology transfer as an instrument to promote friendly relations with the developing countries. In the present context, the US interest in the developing countries and especially India can best be understood as prompted by prospective economic gains from expanding markets for American export. If these economies are developing well they present better chances for consumption of American goods. It also means that the economies would be better organized to supply the imports needed by American industries. Developing economies can also plan an important role as recipients of private investments and as borrowers on American capital market.[3]

In relation to India, the US wished to cultivate a democratic state, based on healthy economy to contain the communist threat. India did not fall in line and gradually there was a decline in the US commitment to India's development. An obvious reason for the low priority given to India in the US aid programmes was India's consistent opposition to military assistance to Pakistan and the other was its policy of non-alignment. Moreover, India adopted restrictive measures in its international trade to promote self-reliance. This lessened the interest of private enterprises in India. In all, India grew marginal to the US interest. The relationship is fairly well described as the United States' "benign neglect" of India. However, India being a developing country with several outstanding features that set it apart from other developing countries cannot be neglected for long. The biggest attraction is India's expanding consumer market. Lately, several agreements were signed between the US and India which show a reawakening of interest in India. In the following pages I would like to briefly dwell on years of Indo-Us technological cooperation so as to be able to sum up how the changing world scenario and India's economic reforms are going to affect the US technology export to India.

Indo-US Economic Relations

US economic aid and assistance played an important role in the development of Indo-US trade and economic relations. American assistance was made available to India under the Point Four Programme through Technical Cooperation Agreements signed between the two countries in December 1950 and January 1952. In eighteen years between 1951 to 1967, through three five year plans the US provided 54.3 per cent of the total foreign aid received by India. During this period the US was the largest donor of foreign aid.[4] The US aid was received for 8 agricultural universities, 12 river valley projects, 5 fertilizer plants, 5 institutes of technology and engineering colleges and several thousands of Indian scientists, engineers, teachers were trained in America.

Evidently, Indo-US economic relationship was a donor-recipient relationship, unacceptable to the Indians as it cast a shadow on the national life and criticized in America as India was seen as an "ungrateful" recipient of aid. India was the largest recipient of the US agricultural commodities under the PL-480 programme. By early seventies the US had also provided 23 per cent of India's total national investment for development of industries in public sector undertakings. The US played an important role in improving the technical know-how of the country and bringing it up-to-date, as well as cooperating in programmes of health, education, and family planning.

Foreign direct investment from the US also aided India's technological growth. It had a positive effect on industrial productivity in India. But the same cannot be said of adaptation of imported technology to Indian conditions. The reason was, very few US subsidiaries and minority companies undertook R & D in the host country. Moreover, package deals for technology transfer were common which did not lead to building up of a technological base in the country. During the late fifties and early sixties, the US branches held significant position, but gradually lost their prominence in India in favour of subsidiaries and minority companies. This was particularly true after the amendment to the Foreign Exchange Regulation Act in 1973.[5] The policies adopted by the Government of India were largely responsible for this change.

Factors Affecting the US Technology Export to India.

The Government of India adopted restrictive and selective approach toward foreign collaborations, an important source of technology import. During the sixties it was felt that foreign collaborations were a net drain on balance of payment and did not lead to absorption of technology as was desired for technological self-reliance of the country. Also, it was felt that outright purchase of technology and licensing of technology were better means of technology import. By the early seventies the policies on foreign investment and technology import acquired a certain clarity. It was realized that India needed technology and not foreign investment. The two issues were linked and resulted in a policy stating that foreign capital was to be allowed only in cases where technology could not be acquired through other means, where export oriented enterprises were to be established, or when foreign exchange for a desired project could not be acquired except through foreign investment. A ceiling of 40% on foreign equity in concerns in India was imposed with a few exceptions, to ensure inflow of sophisticated technology and export promotion.

During the seventies, policies and procedural guidelines for foreign collaboration were laid down. These were the basic tenets for import of technology through foreign collaboration and were enumerated in three illustrative lists of industries specifying the roles allotted to foreign investment with majority participation in each group. The first list enumerated industries where foreign investment would be permitted with or without technical collaboration; the second list contained those where only foreign technical collaboration, and not investment would be permitted, and the third list comprised those where no foreign participation, neither financial nor technical, would be considered necessary. A limit was also placed on royalties payments. Royalty was grouped into two ranges, a low range upto 3% and the other upto 5%.

These policies seemed irrational to the US and protests were heard on rule-bound insistence on sharing of technology and dilution of equity. These policies forced Coca Cola and IBM out of India. As an additional disincentive for investment in India, it took endless time to untie red tape and get projects approved. Then there were difficulties posed by the unions and government officials once the industry was operating.

Several other factors restricting technology flow from the US to India came to the fore during the seventies. To begin with, on the Indian side the US was not thought of as a reliable partner in development due to the US strong-arm tactics of the mid-sixties. Indians recall with bitterness the broken promise of aid to Bokaro Steel Plant made by the Kennedy administration and scuttled by the Congress unwilling to contribute to the building of a socialist public sector.[6] What irked India most was the US attitude of not accepting "significant Indian technical participation in what, for it, was to be a demonstration of American technological superiority in the cold war rivalry with the Soviet Union."[7]

Another irritant affecting the Indo-US technological cooperation was the issue of nuclear fuel supply for Tarapur. India and the US signed a 30 year treaty for nuclear cooperation in 1963.

Under the agreement the US was to supply 14,500 kgs of LEU as fuel for the two light water power reactors at Tarapur. These reactors were supplied by America with safeguards against misuse through independent monitoring. Carter Administration with its commitment to Non-Proliferation Treaty stopped shipment for Tarapur in September 1980. The US emerged as a completely unreliable supplier and as a nation likely to ignore treaty commitments arbitrarily and unilaterally.[8] Fuel supply was resumed through French Government in 1983. But the dissonance was not to end here. One of the two Indian reactors at Tarapur was shut down because of lack of needed parts such as monitors and coolant pumps. The supply was delayed as India refused to abide by comprehensive safeguards required under Nuclear Non-Proliferation Treaty. The US Nuclear Regulatory Commission was reluctant to grant required export license.[9] Finally the nuclear reactor components were supplied based on approval that placed safety above the issue of India's failure to abide by international accords on nuclear policy. Evidently, fear of serious radiation leaks in two American reactors decided for a quick supply of the components.

Another case of considerable importance that affected the Indo-US technological cooperation was the failure of India to procure license for manufacturing F-104 Supersonic starfighter from the US. India had sought this technology to counter the threat posed by Pakistan's acquisition of F-104s from the US but had to finally settle for the Soviet Mig-21.[10]

A point that needs to be emphasized here is that the US has generally adopted a consistent policy that it would not transfer current military technology to any country other than a military ally. Its nuclear non-proliferation stand is only a derivative of this policy. Export control policies of the US on transfer of technologies that could be used for military purposes need to be studied to fully appreciate the restrictions of the outflow of technologies.

American controls of technology export evolved in response to rapid technology developments and due to the national security connotations of their leakage. Export Control Act of 1945 is the foundation of the United States' export control policy. It was followed by the Export Administration Act (EAA) of 1969 and

1972, which was amended once again in 1985 during the Reagan Administration. Under the EAA, the President has the authority to use export controls for foreign policy or national security purposes after considering the impact of these controls on the economy. The Department of Commerce exercises control over strategic commodities and technologies, but must consult with the Department of Defense (DoD) commodities and technologies covered by the provisions of the EAA are generally referred to as "dual use technologies," i.e. technologies for civil use which could be used for military purposes.

A list is maintained by the secretaries of Commerce and Defense covering the "dual use technologies." This is known as the Commodity Control List (CCL). A parallel list of munitions with export controls, known as the US Munitions List is also maintained. Both the Munitions List and the CCL correspond with secret lists developed in consultation with the US allies and are derived from a DoD list of "dual use technologies." This basic list is called the "DoD Militarily Critical Technologies List" (MCTL). All export applications to Department of Commerce are forwarded to the DoD as well as to the State Department. Their evaluation for technology transfer is based on the MCTL.[11] In addition to these domestic legislations, COCOM (Coordinating Committee for Multilateral Export) controls also keep a check on technological leakage from the West. COCOM controls are determined by the US-Japan and the NATO allies, minus Iceland and Spain.

In the US the swing to protectionism has been judged to have grave implications for the US trade balances. It is stated that secrecy and protectionism that existed in the Soviet Union and its affiliates doomed them to lag behind the West. The new strategy proposed for the US is to raise the cost of western technology for anyone who attempts to profit without just compensation to the initial investor or author.[12] Some "dual-use technologies" are also finding way to the market because similar equipments are often available from other foreign based international companies, making the US companies lose business. Lately efforts were being made in the US to remove over a period of three years 40 per cent of the 200,00 items on the list of restricted goods.[13]

Apparently, the US is consolidating its position in technology market as the challenge from Japan and European Economic Community grows. It is important for the US not only to protect its sensitive technologies from leakage but also to get just remuneration for its patents and copyrights. The losses incurred by copyright holders in the US have been much in the focus lately as the Bush administration is committed to get fair returns to its traders.

Indo-US Technological Cooperation in the 1980s

During the 1980s high technology transfer from the US to India increased. This was mainly due to concerted efforts on both sides to improve trade ties. Liberalization of Indian economy has facilitated technology import through foreign direct investment, while Indo-US collaboration for Science and Technology flourished under the three-year Science and Technology Initiative signed by Prime Minister Indira Gandhi and President Reagan in 1982 and renewed in 1985. Cooperation resulting from this agreement is matched only by cooperation and exchanges the US has with a handful of its close allies—countries which are among the most technologically advanced in the world.

Another important basis for the US technology export to India is a memorandum of understanding (MOU) between the two countries, signed in May 1985. The objective of the MOU is to establish a mechanism for the expeditious review of export licence applications for India without jeopardizing the US national security and nuclear non-proliferation interests. The agreement permits the use of sophisticated American technology for Indian business and military ventures.

These agreements emphasize the reawakening of American interest in India. Over two decades of "benign neglect" of India has given way to the US seeking a new role for itself as a dominant economic power in India. As a result of aid cuts in several stages, the US is eventually the ninth most generous donor to India in the non-communist world. Japan is the biggest donor giving twelve times the amount given by Washington in the form of direct loans or grants.[14] Decline in assistance and consequent decline in influence are sought to be mitigated by being more forthcoming on licenses for high technology items in military and other fields.

Another factor promoting India's technology import from the US is that the US is India's biggest source of private foreign investment. As required by India's policies for foreign collaboration, nearly all of foreign direct investment is toward technical collaborations or export oriented industries. To advance technological gains through collaboration of the Indian and the US private sector a Programme for the Advancement of Commercial Technology (PACT) was signed by Indian Ministry of Finance and the US Agency for International Development (USAID) in August 1985. PACT envisages technology development (and not just technology transfer) through Indo-US joint ventures in R & D. It is expected that such joint ventures will not only bring in and introduce new technologies and processes from the US, but also provide the Indian partner an opportunity to acquire the US R & D management techniques.

One could state with some confidence that STI and PACT have been successful in setting the ball rolling for the Indo-US technological cooperation. Science and technology cooperation in "low-visibility" civilian fields does not come across many hurdles. The success of MOU and transfer of dual-use technology is yet a controversial issue.

As seen during the Super Computer deal the US demands to inspect and monitor the end-uses of the facility in order to safeguard against Indian misuses and accessibility to other countries. In some quarters in India, this is seen as a compromise on India's sovereignty. The MOU gets dubbed as "NPT in disguise."[15] It should however, be noted that American high technology export is that of caution even in its dealings with Western allies. These nations also do not have freedom to use them as they want and even to transfer the systems to new sites within their territories.

The Indo-US trade relations are also under strain due to the US decision to include India, along with Japan and Brazil in the Super 301 provisions of the 1988 US Omnibus trade Act. Super 301 affects India's technology import from the US as the US is opposed to Indian import policies that provide for import restrictions and impose export obligations on companies investing in India. Such policies were formulated to promote indigenous technological growth. India was also cited as one of the twelve "problem" countries that failed to provide "adequate and effective" protection for the US copyrighted works or have continued to place unfair barriers to market access for those works. The US also reportedly remained angry with India for blocking the US efforts in the GATT Uruguay Round to protect intellectual property rights.

Conclusions

As transfer of technology takes place, interdependence among nations increases. However, it would be wrong to assume a smooth flow of technology across the national borders. Governments of various countries often control the transborder flow of technology in order to protect declining industries and to promote leading competitive industries. In the case of the US technology, export is further restricted in order to control the outflow of militarily sensitive technologies, thereby adding national security issues to other domestic constraints on technology export.

Although the export control policies of the US regulating transfer of technologies, manufacturing processes and strategic commodities are in reality barriers to free trade, these are also used as levers to advance national interest by linking export decisions with security issues. Technology transfer is also seen as a "penetration mechanism" that advances American foreign policy interests by tying the recipient State to the US for spare parts, training programmes and even long term loans. The fall-out of "penetration mechanism" is restrictions posed by the developing countries to protect their infant economies. Most of the restrictions on import through tied loans or foreign collaboration are imposed by the less developed countries to promote their indigenous technological capabilities, in order to attain self-reliance. India is in the forefront for adopting such restrictive measures.

A change can be seen coming about in the development strategies adopted by the developing countries as the growth of NICs has boosted their confidence in outward oriented development which favours open market economy. India's policies for opening up the economy to finally integrate with the global economy have come into force with a greater impact under P.V. Narasimha Rao Government. Although the stage was set for liberalization in the early 1980s, it is only now that important measures are being taken to speed up the process of globalizing the economy.

These changes call for bold steps to be taken on technology import policy as the pressure is mounting to remove the barriers to foreign collaborations and for a liberal import of capital goods and technology to make Indian industry globally competitive. Steps are already taken towards inviting foreign investment and market is increasingly made attractive by increasing the percentage of equity participation and by allowing the use of trade marks. The process of licensing is streamlined by allowing for automatic permission for foreign technology agreements in high priority industries. This would promote technology import from the US through foreign collaborations. In the coming decade the transfer of technology from the US to India is likely to increase as a result of liberalization of Indian economy. Even with all the constraints the US was the highest investor in India (see table 1). Transfer of technology is further reinforced through the US patents registered with India (see table 2).

Although it is felt that technology transfer is an ineffective tool for foreign policy as it raises hopes of the developing countries which often results in resentment for the supplier country in case of the failure of a suitable technology transfer, it has effectively brought the US and India closer. Closer ties between India and the US are attributed to expanding commercial ties and transfer of technology. Harry Barnes, former ambassador to New Delhi is reported to have convinced the administration about the need for a "a new line to keep India happy without upsetting Pakistan and that the way to do this would be through commerce and the transfer of high-technology."[16]

Indo-US technological cooperation is successful in so far as the number of items requiring a validated license from the US authorities has gone down. The items being licensed are more valuable high-technology commodities. The total value of approved transfer of technology under various heads has also gone up from 374 million in 1986 to 642 million in 1988.[17]

With the US economy facing recession, the US is not in a position to provide with development aid to the developing countries to further its influence to serve national interest. Henry Kissinger once stated, "America's ability to contribute money and run the world in the old-fashioned way of the 1950s and 1960s is now over. What we can contribute—and what the world wants—is our technological capabilities."[18] Evidently, the time has come for the US to make full use of technology to maintain its dominance in the world.

Time is also ripe for India to take a plunge for globalising its economy through increased competitiveness. With the sudden collapse of the Soviet Union India has lost some of its bargaining capacity vis-a-vis the US. This is to India's disadvantage. But India has successfully kept its sources for technology diversified. Although Great Britain and Germany are not the major suppliers of technology through foreign collaborations and patents, these are close competitors (see table 1). Japan is also presently showing more interest in the Indian market. This should strengthen Indian's position in technology import from the developed countries. However, further changes in India's trade and import policies are on the cards.

Furthermore, if India is not to remain a target for unilateral retaliatory actions of an economic power, the solution lies in settling trade and tariff related disputes through multilateral organisations. The developed countries, which account for nearly 90 per cent of the world trade are all ranged against India. Developing countries like Mexico, Brazil and Argentina and the entire ASEAN block have fallen in line with the demands of the developed countries for lowering import controls. In such a situation India has to reconsider its trade and import policies and reach a suitable compromise if it wants to remain on world trade map.

NOTES

1. W.W. Robinson, "Technological Advances—Their Impact on US Foreign Policy Relative to the Developing Countries," in Anne G. Keatley, ed., *Technological Frontiers and Foreign Relations* (New

Delhi: Asian Books, 1987), p. 268.
2. These propositions found expression in 1976 at the fourth meeting of the United Nations Committee on Trade and Development (UNCTAD IV) in Nairobi.
3. The Atlantic Council Working Group on the US and the Developing Countries, *The United States and the Developing Countries* (Boulder, Colorado: Westview, 1977), p. 9.
4. India, Ministry of Finance, Department of Economic Affairs, *Report on the Indo-US Technical Cooperation Programme* (New Delhi: GOI Press, 1957), p. 9.
5. P.C. Roy, *Indo-US Economic Relations* (New Delhi: Deep and Deep, 1980), p. 150.
6. Philip Oldenburg, "India and the United States: Accidental or Inevitable Antagonists?" *Asian Affairs* (Winter 1988-89), p. 224.
7. B.R. Nayar, *India's Quest for Technological Independence*. vol. 1 (New Delhi: Lancers, 1983), p. 217.
8. B.R. Babu, "Domestic Dynamics and Indo-US Relations since 1965: An Analysis," Paper presented at the Conference on Indo-US History of Relations During Last Four Decades, held at India International Centre, New Delhi, January 1991, p. 25.
9. *The New York Times*, 18 June 1983, p. 3.
10. K. Subrahmanyam, "Transfer of Arms and Military Technology as an Instrument of Policy," *Strategic Analysis*, vol. XII, no. 2, May 1987, p. 127.
11. Ashok Raj, "US Hi-Tech Diplomacy and the Indian Super-Computer Deal," *Strategic Analysis*, vol. XI, no. 6 (September 1987), pp. 736-38.
12. Philip A. Roberts, *Technology Transfer: A Policy Model* (Washington D.C.: National Defense Univ. Press, 1988), pp. 18-20.
13. "Easing Technology Restrictions," *Congressional Quarterly Almanac*, 99th Congress, 2nd Session, 1986 (Washington D.C.: C O Inc., 1987), p. 344.
14. *The New York Times*, 21 April 1988, p. 6.
15. For details see, Ashok Raj, pp. 735-53.
16. *The Times of India*, 10 February 1989, p. 14.
17. *Ibid*.
18. Henry R. Nau, *Technology Transfer and United States Foreign Policy* (New York: Praeger, 1976), p. 1.

Research Scholar
University of Bombay

Table 1
Foreign Investment in India during 1986-89
Approvals for top-six investors
Quantum of Investment (Rs. in lakhs)

Country	1986	1987	1988	1989
Australia	56.20	188.00	10.01	300.00
Canada	138.00	275.00	26.00	117.00
F.R.G.	2,015.73	986.915	3,099.90	12,032.85
France	209.82	535.35	1,177.97	845.69
Japan	561.61	690.62	1,742.58	877.93
Netherlands	80.00	100.65	105.30	230.56
Switzerland	475.15	885.30	273.73	774.26
U.K.	771.53	845.10	1,390.75	3,295.40
U.S.A.	2,936.9095	2,951.495	9,713.73	6,215.59
NRI	790.40	2,077.40	1,679.90	2,117.76

Adapted from: Dept. of Industrial Development, *Annual Reports 1986-90*, Ministry for Industrial Development (New Delhi, USG PO, 1986-90).

Table 2
Number of Applications for Patents Filed in India
by Foreign Countries from 1980-81 to 1987-88

Country	80-81	81-82	82-83	83-84	84-85	85-86	86-87	87-88
U.S.A.	570	655	714	894	862	968	857	980
Federal Rep. of Germany	274	229	273	248	289	277	307	305
U.K.	210	233	228	228	244	278	306	257
France	133	128	146	157	168	188	191	171
Japan	96	98	128	99	133	140	135	126
Switzerland	90	72	64	65	135	116	137	109
Italy	77	80	87	51	99	62	67	57
USSR	57	52	37	36	58	68	64	99
Netherlands	50	59	42	42	52	56	73	46
Others	219	271	231	276	335	374	369	407
Total	1776	1877	1950	2090	2320	2527	2506	2527

Source: Dept. of Science and Technology, *Research and Development Statistics*, *1988-89* (New Delhi: GOI, 1990), p. 74.

The U.S. Trade Policy Toward Newly Industrializing Countries

SUNIL SONDHI

There have been major changes in the US trade policies in the 1970s and 1980s. From the end of World War II through the Kennedy Round of trade negotiations in the 1960s, the United States was the world's leader promoting multilateral trade liberalization. This was emphatically not the case in earlier decades. The United States has traditionally been a protectionist, high-tariff country. In 1935 Schattschneider had highlighted the main reason for this protectionism.[1] Producers and workers threatened by free imports tend to be concentrated, organized, and ready and able to press their interests in the political arena. Those who benefit from trade are diffuse, and their stake in any particular trade matter is usually small.

Various factors—the 'lesson' of Great Depression, the Cold War imperative, the US economic dominance and prosperity—contributed to the shift in the US trade policies toward free trade after 1945. But if early postwar years were one of creation, the more recent years have been one of erosion, of relative weakening, which began in the 1970s and accelerated in the 1980s.

Newly Industrializing Countries

There is no clear, unambiguous definition of the 'newly industrializing countries.' Different writers have used different indicators, including level of industrialization, rates of growth and, most frequently, level or rate of growth of manufactured exports. For the top-ranking Asian 'tigers' (South Korea, Hong Kong,

Taiwan and Singapore), and for India, manufactured exports represent 50 percent or more of total exports; for the Latin American (Argentina, Brazil, Mexico) and second-tier Asian NIC's, the figure is lower, between 20 and 40 percent.[2] The countries included here are not meant to represent a definitive list of NIC's but to be indicative of the emerging group of countries that are changing the face of the international economy. There is little doubt about the impact these nations are having on the US and the international economy. The NICs are at the center of policy discussions about trade, debt, technology, foreign investment, and structural adjustment, and their part in these discussions will increase during the 90s.

In the case of the US trade with the newly industrializing countries, three major developments since 1980 together constitute a deepening yet troublesome economic interdependence between the United States and the leading NICs of Asia and Latin America in particular. First, there has been a marked shift in the thrust of expanding exports by developing countries away from the OPEC countries and in favour of the NICs. From 1980 to 1986, the share of world exports held by the OPEC countries dropped from 15.7 percent to 5.8 percent, while the share of world manufactured exports held by other developing countries (mainly NICs) increased from 9 to 13 percent.[3] Secondly, the growth in NIC exports of manufactures since 1980 was accounted for largely by the US market. In 1981 the United States enjoyed a 5 billion surplus in its manufacturing trade; by 1985 this surplus had swung to a 113 billion deficit and in 1986 it increased to over 140 billion. While much of this deficit has been attributed to the rise in the foreign exchange value of the dollar, surge in the NIC exports to the United States during this period was a contributory factor. In 1985 the United States took something in excess of 60 percent of all manufactured exports from the developing countries. Among the other developed countries, Japan's imports of the NIC manufactures increased only marginally from 1981 to 1985, whereas the EEC's imports actually declined during the same period.[4] Thirdly, large and growing US export interests in the NICs proved highly vulnerable to financial and economic conditions in those countries. The US exports to the developing countries declined more than other exports during the five-year period 1980 to 1985. In that period, the US exports to the developing countries fell by 24.4 percent in real terms while the exports to the rest of the world fell by 11.7 percent. Further, the US exports to twenty-one developing countries heavily burdened with debt fell by 31.3 percent in real terms between 1980 and 1984. These figures confirm that the Third World debt has a major impact on the US exports. Decline of the US exports to developing countries during 1980-85 had significant impact on employment in the United States. More than 17 million US jobs were lost due to the recession and debt crisis in the Third World. This represented 21 percent of the official estimates of unemployment in the United States in 1985.[5] These dynamic and at times turbulent developments in the US trade with the NICs led the Reagan and Bush administrations to take an activist approach in foreign trade during the latter half of the 1980s.

The US Policies

The US trade policy toward newly industrialized countries is marked by preferences and interventions in support of bilateral or industry goals. The record of US interventions during the 80s has been largely inconsequential or negative toward the NICs, with the exception of a couple of promising initiatives in the multilateral arena. Bilateral negotiations on import restraints, preferential schemes, and multilateral trade negotiations are discussed below.

During its second term the Reagan administration pursued an active policy of bilateral negotiation and threatened import restraint to achieve greater market access for US exports to specific countries. The NICs have borne the brunt of the countervailing duty and anti-dumping investigations and Section 301 actions against perceived unfair trade practices abroad. Apart from the original Section 301 retaliatory statute, enacted as part of the Trade Act of 1974 and subsequently revised in 1984 and 1988, two new provisions 'Super 301' and 'Special 301' were created by the Omnibus Trade and Competitiveness Act of 1988 to govern comprehensive trade negotiations with selected countries. These provisions allow the US Trade Representative to threaten trading partners with retaliatory sanctions, if they do not alter or eliminate trade policies that are adjudged to violate the United States rights. The USTR is empowered to take all 'appropriate action' to obtain the removal of foreign trade barriers that are deemed to violate the United States trade rights, including the threat and actual imposition of retaliatory tariffs and quotas.

Most developing countries are granted some degree of preferential access to the United States market, through the Generalized System of Preferences (GSP) and/or the Caribbean Basin Initiative (CBI). Both of these programmes were originally intended to provide a sort of free-market form of foreign assistance, by offering non-reciprocal, duty-free treatment for certain qualifying products that the beneficiary countries export. In recent years, however, these programmes have been used as indirect tools by American trade negotiators. The GSP has contained neoreciprocal elements ever since it was renewed by the Trade and Tariff Act of 1984. It now provides that the USTR could threaten countries with the partial loss of GSP privileges on some products, or offer them more secure GSP benefits on others, depending whether or not the country co-operated with the United States. After a general review in 1985-87, the USTR announced that several of the more advanced beneficiary countries (NICs) were losing part of their GSP eligibility, while some others were being rewarded with more secure access under this programme. In making the announcement, the USTR noted that the general review helped to secure improved protection for the United States investment and intellectual property in seven countries and territories in Asia and the Pacific. The GSP programme remains an important form of leverage in the United States trade negotiations. This fact is demonstrated by the magnitude of trade involved: 50.0 billion worth of United States imports from developing countries were eligible for GSP treatment in 1988.[6] The Trade and Competitiveness Act of 1988 authorized the President to remove a beneficiary country's CBI privileges on a product-specific basis, if he finds that the country no longer meets its designation requirements. The CBI is now equally useful to the United States negotiators as a means of pressuring the beneficiary countries.

In September 1986, the GATT Contracting Parties met in Uruguay to launch the eight postwar round of multilateral trade negotiations. Two aspects of the new round stand out. The agenda is longer and more complex than for previous rounds. The issues include traditional industrial tariff and institutional matters, more recent concern with nontariff measures including standstill and rollback of existing quota restrictions, and largely new issues such as agriculture, services, intellectual property, and trade-related investment measures. Second, the active participants are more numerous and now include many newly industrializing countries. Unlike the pattern of previous rounds, developing countries played a key role in launching the new round, acting through various groupings some of which cut across traditional North-South lines.

The United States negotiating objectives in the Uruguay Round are established in three distinct documents: the Reagan administration's 1986 paper on intellectual property policy, the formal expression of negotiating objectives in the Trade and Competitiveness Act of 1988, and the proposal advanced by the United States delegation to the Uruguay Round talks in 1987 (together with subsequent submissions expanding upon these views). As presented in these documents the United States goal is to make trade related intellectual property and investment measures an integral element in the international trading system, and to legitimize the linkage between these issues and trade in goods. The centerpiece is a proposed multilateral agreement that would require all signatories to agree inter alia to create an effective economic deterrent to international trade in goods and services which violates intellectual property rights and prevents foreign investment.

In effect, such an agreement would oblige other GATT members to protect American intellectual property and investment, define the terms under which this protection must be extended, and ratify the United States policy of threatening retaliation against countries that violate these rights. The implicit bargain offered by the United States is that, in exchange for a commitment on the issues of intellectual property, investment, services, and agriculture, the United States will further reduce its trade barriers, and may agree to refrain from taking unilateral action against its trading partners.

With the exception of the successful inauguration of the Uruguay Round negotiations, almost all the major trade initiatives during the 80s represented either increased barriers to trade or discriminatory reductions in trade barriers. An effective argument used in lobbying for protectionism was that unfair trade practices by other countries were a major cause of the US trade deficits. It had the appeal of diverting attention from any domestic factors that might explain the US competitiveness problem, and of enabling public and private officials still to maintain that they favoured free trade. They maintained that this trade must be fair as well as free, however. More and more members of the Congress began to adopt the view that the unwillingness of foreign governments to open their domestic markets was a major cause of the US trade problem. Blaming foreigners did not involve the risk of voter disapproval that raising taxes or cutting social or defense expenditures did. The fact that the administration had not made widespread use of this argument also made it attractive as a way of shifting blame for the trade deficit problem from the Congress to the administration.[7]

NIC Response

The newly industrializing countries present an increasingly important challenge to the US trade policies. These countries hold a status between the other industrialized countries which are in agreement with the US on several issues, and the less developed countries which pose no significant challenge to the US policies. The technological base of the NICs is advancing, and their industries are becoming more competitive, while the United States undergoes a relative erosion in its technological, competitive, and trade advantages. The advancement of the NICs can be attributed in some measure to their adoption of foreign technology, which involves, from the US point of view, unfair trade practices and intellectual property violations. It is in the interest of the NICs not to accept new and stricter intellectual property and trade regimes. This conflict of interests is a replay of the all-too-familiar nineteenth century act on free trade. The nineteenth century was characterized by major policy conflicts among the pioneer country in industrialization (Great Britain) and the other newly industrializing countries (United States, France, Germany, etc.). The former preached 'free trade' in all goods, because of its early industrialization, in which it had achieved a comparative cost advantage. Those NICs responded at that time by adopting protective policies for the development of their 'infant' industries. Brazil, India, Argentina, Egypt, and Yugoslavia currently lead the newly industrializing countries which are strongly opposed to progress on new issues in the Uruguay Round—services, investment, and intellectual property. They argue instead for immediate implementation of the standstill and rollback commitment in the Punta Declaration on all trade-restricting measures affecting manufactured goods and agriculture.

At the bilateral level, however, the conflict between the US and the NICs positions is not so sharp. The response of several newly industrializing countries in their bilateral negotiations with the United States has helped to reduce mutual differences. Argentina, Mexico, Korea, and Taiwan were the major NICs which successfully negotiated with the United States during 1989-90, after they were placed on priority watch list by the USTR in 1989 for violating intellectual property rights or unfair trade practices. More recently, in January 1992, China and the United States reached an agreement in a contentious trade dispute involving protection of American copyrights and patents. The US trade officials had called China the 'single largest pirator worldwide of US copyrights,' and American business leaders had alleged that they had lost 430 million annually from Chinese copyright violations on everything from drugs and computer programmes to clothing and records.[8]

These bilateral negotiations and agreements indicate the evolving interest of the newly industrializing countries in intellectual property and foreign investment. To the extent that certain industries within these countries reach more advanced stages, they can be expected to formulate laws that protect intellectual property and foreign investment. The NICs might also view these measures as a means of preserving their own emerging status as exporters of manufactured goods. If the less developed countries are permitted to adopt their technologies and restrict their exports, then further advancement of the NICs may be threatened. The United States is in a position to alter the benefits and costs that the NICs perceive in promoting foreign investment and protecting intellectual property. It is using that position to make the NICs join, not jeopardize the OECD nexus.

Conclusion

The sharp increase in the US trade deficit in the early 1980s changed trade policy from being a matter of concern to only a small number of industries into being a matter of national concern. This development gave impetus to the view that unfair actions by the US trade partners, particularly the NICs, affected almost all industries in the United States and were a major cause of the massive US trade deficit. Emphasis shifted from the view that unfair foreign measures were a major cause of import surges to the view that these measures were a major cause of the US competitiveness problem. Consequently, there were series of bilateral efforts to open the markets of the NICs. The US Congress mandated a tougher approach in the Trade and Competitiveness Act. At the Uruguay Round negotiations the United States has maintained that GATT should include services and intellectual property regimes.

Changes in the US and the NIC's trade policies during the 80s have caused a metamorphosis of global trading regimes. The shift is clearly in the direction of negotiated market shares, bilateral bargaining, and conditional preferential schemes. These more nationalistic approaches to international trade are displacing to a certain degree the basic GATT principles of nondiscrimination, multilateralism, and the unconditional most-favored -nation principle as the governing features of the international political economy.[9] The United States and the NICs are fashioning a new interlocking network of bilateral and regional relationships in which the newly industrializing countries are being coopted as newly influential countries in the global economy and polity.

NOTES

1. E.E. Schattschneider, *Politics, Pressures and the Tariffs* (New York: Prentice-Hall, 1935).
2. Henry R. Nau, "The NICs in a New Trade Round," in Ernest H. Preeg, ed., *Hard Bargaining Ahead* (Washington, DC: Overseas Development Council, 1985), p. 65.
3. Anne O. Krueger, "Trends in the Trade Policies of Developing Countries," in Charles S. Pearson and James Riedel, eds., *The Direction of Trade Policy* (Cambridge, Mass.: Basil Blackwell, 1990), pp. 90-94.
4. Daniel F. Burton, Jr., "International Pressures and Policy Choices," in Thornton F. Bradshaw, et al, eds., *America's New Competitors* (Cambridge, Mass.: Ballinger, 1988), pp. 241-43.
5. John W. Sewell and Stuart K. Tucker, "Swamped by Debt: US Trade with the NICs," in Bradshaw, p. 189.
6. UNCTAD, *Uruguay Round: Further Papers on Selected Issues* (New York: United Nations, 1990), p. 111.
7. Robert E. Baldwin, "US Trade Policy, 1945-1988: From Foreign Policy to Domestic Policy," in Pearson and Riedel, p. 21.
8. "US, China accord on copyrights," *Times of India*, 18 January 1992.
9. Raymond Vernon and Debora Spar, *Beyond Globalism* (New York: Free Press, 1989).

Rajdhani College
University of Delhi

America in the 70s-80s: Human Rights Perspective

DIPANKAR BASU

In any discussion on America in the 70s-80s from the viewpoint of "Human Rights," certain questions arise in our mind.

What is 'Human Rights?' What is the purpose of Human Rights debate and its relation to political behaviour in the U.S.A.? How far the 'Human Rights Principles' had affected the formulation and implementation of domestic and foreign policies of the U.S., especially in the 70s-80s. Had it been possible for the U.S. to fulfil the Human Rights objectives?

There are other questions also—what priority Human Rights can command on foreign policy agenda and whether such policies can claim to be consistent in the world of states and of "East-West super power" relations? How far the U.S. Aids were influenced by Human Rights considerations? How can universalistic Human Rights be incorporated in the foreign policy of the US? How far the tenets of Human Rights had been implemented within the U.S. itself?

Answer to all these questions depend to a great extent, on how we define Human Rights. Human Rights, in general, deal with rights of human beings—something humane or humanitarian in character, and the rights necessary for the mankind.

All of us belong to one family: mankind. Each member of the family has the same fundamental and equal rights. Each of us is entitled to have all of these rights respected. At the same time it is our responsibility to protect those rights for all others. We all agree that differences of race, sex, language, religion, social origin, political ideas, differences of property and others do not change these rights. In brief, every person, regardless of who he is and what he does or thinks is born with Human Rights.

The debate about definitions of Human Rights is crucial in order to understand the division between states over the importance to be given to economic and social rights, as opposed to civil and political rights. At the same time all these rights are self-generating and they need legislation, promotion and protection—which on the other requires resources. But the point is that Human Rights are assorted in a world, in which there are shortages, both of motivation for forbearances and of resources.

It is also that everyday these rights are being violated in country after country, and such violation whenever it occurs is a threat to the welfare and dignity of the entire community or humanity. The protection of Human Rights, therefore is a world wide responsibility, and such belief has given birth to the international struggle for Human Rights.

The principle of Human Rights has also become one of the important issues of the Post-war period, from the perspectives of both Universalism and particularism. The idea of Universal Human Rights meets the need of human beings so as to establish a moral basis for politics. So the search for a Universal, ideal, even in the U.S.A., had increased specially for the last forty years, in spite of questions of definition and applicability.

But there are obstacles to universalisation of Human Rights, as great purposes of the state—even in the U.S.—are security, welfare of its citizens, international trade and others: neither of these could be advanced by paying attention to Human Rights principles. For example, the U.S. had to maintain relations with regimes in spite of their violations of Human Rights, like Philipines under Marcos or Iran under Shah.

In this context, it is to be noted that the Third World countries have stressed the importance of socio-economic rights, Right to Self-Determination, Right to Food, Right to Peace, Right to Development and others. They have also stressed for a new 'International Economic Order' and to have a restructuring of the world economy on the basis of a dialogue between the North and the South, the East and the West. Declaration on the Right to Development, now before the U.N., was also made in 1985, as a right of both the individual and the people.

At the same time a number of less developed countries play down the importance of Human Rights in their own domestic policies, arguing that threats to security justify restrictions on Human Rights.

An important belief in the modern world is that while we may not be able to find a Universal definition of Human Rights all of us still recognise violations when they occur whether within or outside a country. But then it is difficult to persuade the officials to support the case for Human Rights and even more so to stop Human Rights violations. It is necessary to put constant pressure on Governments to act, as without that pressure, Governments would do little.

It is also difficult to categorize Human Rights, as some are self-regarding and others one other-regarding, however, both of these raise issues of freedom from oppression and of the role of Governments. Difficulties also arise as and when we try to broaden the concept of rights from individual to collective rights and from negative to positive rights.

Previously perceptions of Human Rights at the International level tended to concentrate on treaties for the protection of minorities rather than on rights which related to the whole of mankind. However, at present Human Rights remain a key factor in the current understanding of relations between the states.

As we refer to Human Rights we refer to global society or a society of mankind. When we refer to foreign policy and consider the world of states, then we are making distinctions between groups of people and their conflicting interests, which divide them. One can say that the best way to solve the dispute between Human Rights and formulation of foreign policy, say in the U.S.A., would be to forget about the issue of Human Rights completely, as exemplified in some aspects of the Debate. But in practice, separation of Human Rights or its elimination from foreign policy could not be made, even in the U.S.A., since the humanitarians and the people of country would not have allowed to do so. Public opinion, even in the U.S. will ensure that Human Rights are in the forefront. International conventions and International law would always force foreign ministries or the diplomats, to pay attention to what is happening on Human Rights in the

International community.

From the viewpoint of a diplomat Human Rights serve to obstruct system of communication, which is necessary for diplomacy between the states and so should not be allowed to undermine the traditional state system. But the diplomats need to be concerned with Human Rights also.

In the eyes of realists, like President Nixon or Henry Kissinger, morality and foreign policy coexist uneasily—conflicts between Morality and Reality so continue even in the field of International Relations.

Human beings live in societies and want to enjoy rights within the societies. Morality, Humanitarianism and Politics are intertwined—for example, humanitarian concern over famine or food aid as against legal concern over torture. Food and torture represent two opposing dilemmas. From the viewpoint of Human Rights moralists, universal morality of the human community can be set against that of morality of the states—this means Human Rights can challenge jurisdiction of the states. Rights themselves exist in the moral bases of human community—it is the way they are implemented which is a question of politics.

The interpretation of Human Rights principles is not simple and will differ both in different places and over time—nevertheless we cannot avoid passing judgements. The question of judgement also raises another issue regarding universality i.e. whether everyone agrees that a particular phenomenon is a Human Right. Here again all cultures are not in agreement. In the liberal tradition of the U.S. the issue is not whether everybody agrees that right exists, but whether everyone ought to do so. What universalism establishes is a higher court of appeal against abuses by Sovereign powers in dealing with their citizens. At the same time lack of "International Policing" stands in the way of Universality of Human Rights. In this connection, it can be questioned as to whether the U.S. could have had the right to act as an International guardian in this respect.

Prevention of abuses of Human Rights also calls for specific education in these issues. There is a need to have "Preventive strategies," which again depend upon education to ignorance, and creation of consciousness about the Human Rights.

Since 1945, extension of the nation of Universal Human Rights has been effected through the Preamble of the U.N. charter, through the U.N. Declaration of Human Rights in the General Assembly on 10th December, 1948, International covenant of Economic, Social and Cultural Rights, International covenant on Civil and Political Rights of 1976, Helsinki Declaration of 1975, Madrid Conference of 1983 and others. But no headway has been made, specially at super power levels or in relation between the East and the West.

However evolutions of Human Rights had been subject to a number of considerations. First, that the term Human Rights has not been defined specifically by the U.N. Charter and that Human Rights principles were never elaborated. It may be that International Bill of Human Rights and similar other Acts had made some of the contents of the term more explicit, but Human Rights still remain relative in nature. Secondly, Human Rights are often involved in the pursuit of politics rather than per se and so Human Rights became an instrument of Government and foreign policy. Thirdly, because Human Rights are linked to other interests, it is not surprising to find double standards at work. Finally, Human Rights may themselves be in conflict, like between individual and collective Rights. The question is how to reach a compromise between various Human Rights—this poses a continual dilemma at the International and national levels. Problems of Human Rights are also to be judged from the viewpoint of deductive or inductive; International or national; First World or Third World; Collective or Individual; majority or minority; mobility or immobility; prevention or cure; civil and political or economic, social and cultural; standard setting or norm setting at International level. There is no doubt that there is a need to have an appreciation of local and national principles and practices, especially in developing countries, which may contribute to international norm creation. A country's perception of Human Rights, moreover may differ at the national and international levels—because of expediency and foreign policy concerns, but few countries could deny the existence of Right of Self-Determination in International Law.

It has also been observed that the mere fact that certain

countries deny the binding force of Human Rights treaties, does not imply that these countries disregard all the Human Rights principles propounded by such treaties.

With these ideas in mind, we can study the Human Rights perspectives in America in the 70s-80s.

The ideas of Human Rights, specially those regarding Justice, Equality before the law, individual freedom and liberty have occupied important positions in the U.S. since the founding of American colonies. This can be seen by an examination of various documents in American History, in American patriotic rituals and speeches; in the Decalaration of Independence of July 1776, in the preamble of the USA's constitution of 1787 (which proclaims that among its purposes one is to establish justice and to secure the blessings of Liberty to ourselves and our posterity) and others. The statue of Liberty in New York Harbour also welcomes the people of the world to the Land of Freedom. The National anthem of the U.S. (Star spangled Bamna) also refers to the U.S. of the land of the free and the home of the brave. The pledge of Allegiance, a patriotic ritual performed in many schoolrooms of the U.S.A. also defines the U.S. as delivering liberty and justice for all.

In a speech delivered on 6th December 1978, in commemoration of the 30th Anniversary of the U.N. sponsored universal declaration of Human Rights, Mr. Jimmy Carter, the 39th President of the U.S. who also made important campaign towards Human Rights, during the 1970s-80s states: "Human Right is the soul of own foreign policy, because Human Right is the very soul of our sense of nationhood." It is to be noted that in the domain of political ideas of America in the 70s-80s, there were two important changes—first there was the decline of the Ideas of New Deal as the principal idea of American political life. Secondly, there was a new emphasis on the value of participation in politics.

It is also that the national political institutions of the U.S. (with the presidency congress, Supreme Court) and the extra-constitutional political institutions (like the political parties, the electorate) have changed—all of these had influenced the ideas of Human Rights in the U.S.A. during the 70s-80s.

Moreover, the idea of politics of coalition building constructive coalition between the Republicans and the Southern Democrats in the Congress or the New Deal coalition of White Southerners and Blocks of urban working electorate, and soon gave way to a politics of majority creation in America of the 70s-80s—may be because of an absence of crisis. It was expected that in the event of any crisis, domestic or international, social or economic, a new stable structure and alignments would develop as also the possibility of a New Political Philosophy.

In America the 70s-80s was also a period of the end of cold war and the rise of Detente—from Ideal politik to real politik, disengagement from Vietnam, Detente with China, Arms control as an important factor of Detente trade and technology being used as incentives for Soviet self-containment, an erosion of U.S. Alliances, and at the same time disillusionment with Detente. It was also a period when there was a search of consensus and Human Rights.

But with the Cold War anti-Communist Consensus being disintegrated in Vietnam, and the U.S. being tired of the new role as World's policeman, President Nixon and his Secretary of State Kissinger abandoned the missionary style and the moralistic justification of foreign policy. Kissinger emphasized on States and their legitimate interests rather than on moral causes and the division of the world into saints and devils. This no doubt, brought about a clear-cut distinction between the U.S.'s foreign and domestic policies, specially with regards to Human Rights vis-a-vis the U.S. Foreign Policy.

Nixon and Kissinger were clever enough not to publicly condemn other regimes for their violation of Human Rights. Due to this they gained greater concessions from Moscow on Human Rights, including emigration from Soviet Union for the dissidents and the Jews.

To President Nixon and later on President Ford the emphasis on Human Rights was mainly based on private talks, secret diplomacy, pressures and negotiations, without holding offending regime to public condemnation and thus sought to bring about practical results in the American interests. It was thought that normally short of overthrowing a regime, not much can be done about that State's disregard of Human Rights. Critics also pointed out that what the U.S. could do where suppression of political rights was at the heart of a political system of a country, fingers being pointed towards the Soviet Union.

It was Mr. Jimmy Carter, sworn in as the 39th President of the U.S., on 20th Jan. 1977, who sought a consensus in America's self-proclaimed role as "Defender of Democracy and Individual liberty." Human Rights became the platform on which Carter expected to mobilise popular support. Jimmy Carter, a devout Christian, became the "Saviour" of American liberal tradition, which it was alleged Kissinger had abandoned in favour of amoral geopolitics. The U.S. and its people, under Carter, once again stood for something, having reclaimed its democratic heritage also to have a moral basis for its foreign policy. During the Carter era, the U.S. policy was: because we are free, we can never be indifferent to the fate of freedom elsewhere. Our moral sense dictates a clearcut preference for these societies which share with us an abiding respect for individual Human Rights—our commitment to Human Rights must be absolute. Carter Administration also had, through its Human Rights Bureau, an institutional focus for Human Rights. In brief, during the Carter era, Human Right became intertwined with foreign policy issues, specially in the fields of the East-West relations.

However, Carter's policy on Human Rights ran into trouble, specially with regards to the Soviet Union, who did not care for Carter's emphasis on Human Rights, which the Soviets felt was specifically directed against them. Then again, the Soviets interpreted political opposition, freedom of Assembly, freedom of speech and others which were important tenets of Human Rights as danger to their system and 'Counter revolutionary.' Even Carter's policy and support for the Soviet dissidents were viewed by the Soviet Union as a fundamental attempt to undermine the Soviet system.

Carter, on assuming office announced the withdrawal of the U.S. ground forces from South Korea, a decision influenced by South Korea's poor Human Rights record. However, later on he withdrew this: maybe because of Japan's concern for its security as against North Korea, or maybe it was realised that South

Korea feeling abandoned by its protector might violate more Human Rights as its sense of insecurity arose. It is also that for American security and the Human Rights of individuals living under despotic regimes, the wisdom of Carter administration's policy on Human Rights was questioned.

Some critics even suggested that because the U.S. could apply sanctions for violation of Human Rights easily to its friends and allies than its adversaries the policy was applied more frequently to friendly countries, who were generally aligned with the U.S. foreign policy. It was so pointed out that Carter's policy based on Human Rights might be an admirable policy as and when the U.S. efforts made some countries more democratic and respectful of the principles of Human Rights. But in Iran the U.S. policy to establish more Westward looking Democrats, instead of Shah of Iran, failed with the establishment of Islamic theocracy. The U.S.'s policy also failed in Cambodia, where 2 million people out of a population of 8 million died due to Human Rights violation.

It was then questioned as to how far by ignoring the consequences for American security, the respect for Human Rights had been informed by various political changes—like shifting from one regime to another, as in Nicaragua, from the U.S. viewpoint. Critics also observed that American Human Rights policy might lead the U.S., on occasion to topple friendly dictators by not supporting them and thus endangering strategic interests of the U.S. In brief it was realised that the U.S. leverage to shape other regimes was rather limited—specially when it was realised that there could never be certainty about who would be part of the successor's regime or what policies it would follow.

A further result of the emphasis on Human Rights in America during the 70s–80s was also exposed in America's double standard of judgement—say, how could President Carter support his Human Rights stand with his strategic interests in normalizing relations with communist China or what about turning down by Carter of Human Rights (Achievements) infringements by the Soviet Union so as to complete Salt II negotiations or what about his pre-1979 support for Shah of Iran or Carter's visit to South Korea in spite of his earlier criticism.

It can be said that during this period the American Administration failed to decide whether to give priority to Human Rights or to security, specially where a conflict as between these values meant that the pursuit of both enhanced neither.

It had also been observed that the counterperiod suggested a kind of cultural arrogance based on assumption that the American concept of Human Rights was the correct standard for all other countries. Moreover, it was also pointed out that the U.S.'s concern on Human Rights was a revival of the old idea of American "Global Policeman Role"—one crusade being substituted by another. This is not just to criticise the U.S. policy with regards to Human Rights principles, as these principles had always expressed the U.S.'s commitment to values upon which the U.S. was formed. On the other hand it was generally accepted that the U.S. could not pursue Human Rights principles, as a factor of its policy, regardless of their consequences, because they might not support the U.S. interests.

Carter also tried to separate Human Rights from American-Soviet conflict and implement it in less developed countries, where the majority of humanity lived. In the new emerging interdependent world Carter's focus was on the relationship between the Western Industrial democracies and the poor Third World, to create a peaceful World order, based on Human Rights.

After Carter, it was Ronald Reagan, the 40th President of the U.S.A. a conservative, who reunited anti-communism and Human Rights at first—in support of rightwing regimes that ignored Human Rights but then to help transform a number of them into democracies. In the 1980s in spite of serious pressure on the Soviet Union by the U.S no fundamental changes took place in Human Rights policy in the Soviet Union. The expectations that the Soviet Union would follow Helsinki principles were unrealistic as the Soviet attitudes were opportunistic in nature, mainly to have trade access to Western technology crucial for the Soviet economy—maybe there was fall in number of arrests of dissidents but nothing much changed with regards to the Soviet policies and attitudes, towards Human Rights. So the conflicts between the East and the West over the question of Human Rights remained.

George Bush, the 41st President of the U.S.A. since January 1989, followed the policies of Reagan in his first year of administration, maybe with changes here and there. He was of course helped to a great extent by announcement of policies of "Glasnost and Perestroika" by Gorbachev—and that brought about an openness in the field of Human Rights also, vis-a-vis the U.S. and other countries also. This also helped the American administration to tighten its grip over violators of Human Rights, especially through "Economic Aid."

Moreover, the complex international network of political, economic or social agencies of the U.N. and their activities assisted the U.S. in adjusting its national policies peacefully without the various aspirations and needs of different states and thus creating a community of National interests, as the least safeguard of International law. Of course it is true that the larger share of the U.S. foreign economic assistance was carried out through bilateral agreements between the U.S. and the recipient countries. The U.S. had carried out Human Rights ideas into their relations with the Third World through "trade and aid policies." But the question in America in the 70s-80s was whether "Aid" helped development or served other interests including foreign policy ones. So although Carter Administration promoted Human Rights in its foreign policy matters, many right-of-centre but friendly regimes continued to receive aid and only a handful of countries like Argentina, Uruguay, and Ethiopia suffered reduction in aid.

President George Bush also took measures to curtail economic and, in cases of violation of Human Rights by the other states, but often, it had been observed, there was more concern for national security and national interest, rather than on Universal Human Rights.

It is pointed out that the U.S. had historically explained its international commitments in terms of defense of Human Rights as against the onslaught of undemocratic and anti-democratic regimes, as could be traced during the first phase of cold war, when the anti-communism inherent in the containment policy was legitimized by liberal administration of Truman, Kennedy, and Johnson who were also concerned about the Human Rights, as were their successors.

But to many, the proclamation of lofty principles of Human Rights have never been transformed into actuality in the U.S. So in spite of the official self-justification and identification of the U.S. with the principles of Human Rights, it was unlikely that the U.S. could possibly meet the promise of its self-proclaimed standards. So there was a continuous tension between the high standards of American idealism and the reality of continuing abuses in the Civil liberties and other areas.

In the 1970s, in the wake of Watergate scandal during Nixon's Presidency, the Americans were shocked to know that the FBI had been operating for decades, as a secret semi-legal, semi-vigilant political police, conducting massive investigations into various lawful and private activities of Americans, without any legal authority or power to do so, whether by opening mail, or by wire tapping phones and even conducting burglaries.

A Committee of the U.S. Senate also reported in 1976 that such FBI abuses along with similar activities by the CIA and Army Intelligence can go a long way to criticise as a "totalitarian regime." It also appears that the American officials responsible for supervising these agencies and others had shown a great disregard of activities that even threatened the U.S. constitutional system—think of the U.S. role in Nicaragua or in Iran. There is no doubt that there had been a tension between "Ideals" and "Reality" as events of 1970s-1980s can go to prove—both within and outside the U.S. and also with regards to the U.S. and its allies or even in respect of the U.S.'s foreign policy.

The U.S.A.'s role in Panama, Grenada, Nicaragua, Iran and its apparent support to many military dictatorships, the activities of Israel against the Palestinians, also put the U.S., according to critics, on the same level like the other violators of Human Rights. It can also be said that the U.S. had failed to fulfil its promise in Human Rights, from the viewpoint of American self-proclaimed high standards.

On the other hand, the U.S. officials, during the 1970s-80s, concluded that by defending Human Rights at home and abroad, the U.S.A. was being true to itself (and its whole history since 1976). It was pointed out during this period, that the Human

Rights provisions of the Helsinki Final Act were given strong support; democratic regimes were established in Peru, Equador, and Bolivia; American convention on Human Rights came into force and the Inter-American court of Human Rights was established, a new process of illustration process was inaugurated in a number of countries; and in a large number of countries the U.S. undertook various diplomatic interventions, both to remind Governments of its continued concern about general Human Rights conditions and also to seek relief for the sufferers.

On December 10, 1981, the U.S. State department sworn in a new U.S. Assistant Secretary of State for Human Rights, Elliot Abrams, underlying on the Human Rights Day the continuing dedication of the American government and its people to promotion of individual rights of the individual, wherever he or she may live.

In reality, the actual state of Human Rights in the U.S.A. has to be determined by a variety of complex factors and influences like the written constitution, legal principles and statute, judicial interpretation of the constitution laws, and various official orders; the agencies of Public Opinion, the attitudes of policy makers both regarding domestic and foreign policies and the opinion of the elites; and the actions and behaviour of the law-enforcing authorities, including the Judges and others.

It has been observed that in spite of various legal and non-legal protective measures adopted by the U.S. Government, there had been failures specially in case of "Racial Discrimination" or in area of "Due Process of Law" (procedural fairness) or in other areas. In spite of serious attempts to eradicate racial discrimination, there was still a stigma of human injustice in the racial area.

In area of "Due Process of Law," the American police long enjoyed a reputation for violence. No other democratic country accepts and glorifies violence as a way to solve problems, as is done in the U.S.A.; maybe the American society provides the measured climate to do so by the American police.

In the economic and social fields, injustice still remained. In November 1978, out of total unemployment of 5.8% in the U.S.A., the black unemployment (of African Americans) was

11.8%, that is thrice that of the whites—unemployment rate of black teenagers was 36.2% compared to total teenage unemployment of 16.2%. Median Black family income was only 65% of the Median white family income in 1976; and the blacks owned only 1.2% of the business equity and one-tenth of 1% of the value of all stock holding in 1974.

To some, the American records in the field of Human Rights were not as good as the high ideals of the Americans. Of course it can be said that the American record compares favourably with vast majority of nations of the world but it would be a great mistake to be complacent as ideas of Human Rights can rarely be fully satisfied. It is also time that the U.S. Supreme Court and the agencies of Public Opinion had played an important part in the protection of Human Rights—specially in the field of civil liberties.

There is no doubt that American ideals of Human Rights and their application, from the viewpoint of morality and reality, both within and outside the country, had a profound impact upon the world. It is to be seen whether, in a world of International cooperation and peace, the American reality can be closer to the ideals of Human Rights.

Following John Gunther's questions: who runs this place? Who is in charge?—the answer might be: "No one." "Nobody is in charge here." But even then in spite of various causes for dejection, the U.S. had shown considerable capacity for running itself for more than 200 years and is likely to endure for a good deal longer.

Mr. Elliott Abrans, the first U.S. Assistant Secretary for Human Rights laid down in 1981 that two points were important: "first is that we must till the truth" in broadening human rights around the globe and secondly that "it is a moral as well as a statutory obligation."

The choice of techniques for remedial action should however, be made with a practical goal in mind—the main objective ought to be "How can we help to expand the frontiers of liberty or for that matter the Human Rights by an inch or by a mile"?

Darjeeling Government College
Darjeeling

American Approach to Regimes: A Critique of Nuclear Non-Proliferation Regime

UJJWAL K. CHOWDHURY

A less dramatic indicator of the trend in re-structuring the biop-lar security order is the gradual strengthening of incipient regional security arrangements around the Third World. Alongside, there continue the globalist security strategies—initiated and institutionalised in the heyday of bioplarism though radical alterations are affecting them. At both these levels of analysis, attempts of regime-creation are clearly discernible.

In this background, we put forward three purposes in this paper: (a) examining the American approach towards the theory of regime-building; (b) critically examining the existing Global Nuclear Non-Proliferation Regime; and (c) discussing a possible alternative Nuclear Elimination Regime.

American Approach towards the Theory of International Regimes

To begin with, international theory is that part of the study of international relations (IR) which offers descriptive and explanatory statements about patterns, regularities and changes in the structural properties and processes of international systems and their major component units. It is concerned with classes of events (typical behaviour and trends), not with specific occurrences.

Coming specifically to the growing sub-field of the theoretical and empirical studies in international co-operation, the conflict co-operation spectrum of IR appears to be in a continuum, with the global indicator moving gradually towards further co-operation, more categorically at the regional levels. This is unfolding in a transforming pluralistic, multipolar world of increasingly de-ideologised international diplomacy, and in which economic, ecological and demographic imperatives of development are assuming greater significance than the old-fashioned politico-strategic determinants of power.

In the particular case of the American thinking on international co-operation, the impact of behaviouralism has brought a considerably open perspective (in contrast to the previous committed British writings) which is less influenced by a particular historical experience and more concerned to discover explanations for cooperative behaviour in IR, whatever be its source or motive. The major/minor American schools of thought on international co-operation can be chronologically listed as below:

	Name of the Approach	Main Advocates	Decade
1.	Legal Approach	G. Clark & L. Sohn	1950s
2.	Transactionalism	K. Deutsch & D. Puchala	1950s
3.	Pluralism	Conn and Elds	1960s
4.	Neo-functionalism	Ernst Hass, Lindbeng Scheingold & Joseph Nye	1960s & 1970s
5.	Interdependence approach	Robert Keohane & Nye	1970s
6.	International Regimes	Stephen Krasner & others	1980s

For the sake of our analysis here, we are selecting only the Regime Theory. The concept of international regimes, first referred to by Keohane and Nye, has proven its values, identifying important phenomena to be explained and clustering them together. It has served as a label for identifying patterns of what John Ruggie has called "institutionalised collective behaviour" on a variety of subjects.

From predominantly economic issues, it has been extended to include the analysis of international security issues as well. A wide consensus has been reached for a definition of international regimes as principles, rules, norms and procedures around which expectations converge in a given area of IR.

Problems exist in operationalizing this definition; in particular, when the concept of international regime is extended beyond the internationalised results if former interstate agreements, the boundaries between the regime and the non-regime situations become somewhat indistinct.

Regimes have been found to be the intervening variables standing between basic casual factors, on the one hand, and related patterned outcomes and behaviour, on the other. The principles in regimes refer to the beliefs of facts, causation and rectitude. Norms cater to standards of behaviour defined in terms of rights and obligations. Rules are the mutually concluded specific prescriptions or proscriptions for actions. Decision-making procedures in case of regimes refer to the prevailing practices for making and implementing congenial collective choice/action. In this context, confusing regimes with international agreements is a common error. Agreements are adhoc, often 'one shot' arrangements, while regimes are more long-standing arrangements which facilitate agreements, and such agreements, later reinforce existing regimes. Regime-governed behaviour must not be based solely on short-term calculations of interest, but rather on long-term utility maximizing behaviour on the part of the cooperating states through more established and agreeable principles, like Reciprocity.

The normal basic causal factors motivating states to proceed towards regime-formations are: egoistic self-interest, political power, norms and principles, usage and custom, and knowledge. It has also been observed that regime-formation follows three usual paths: (1) *Spontaneous*: in which the regimes emerge almost automatically from the converging expectations of the interacting actors and their actions; (2) *Negotiated*: in which regimes are formed through formal negotiations and explicit agreements; and (3) *Imposed*: in which regimes are, at least initially, forced upon the actors by external imposition.

The literature on regimes also refers to changes in regimes and the creation of pre-change tensions in regimes. The three sources of pressures for regime changes are identified to be: (a) internal contradictions in the sphere of the regime constructed; (b) perceptible shifts in the underlying power-structures based on which the regime has been created; and (c) certain exogenous changes necessitating radical intra-regime changes.

Regimes may vary over time and vary across cases in at least four ways: strength, organizational form, scopes and modes of allocation. The strength of the regime is measured by the degree of compliance with regime injunctions, particularly when the short-term self interest collide with the regime rules. The idea of the organizational form emanates from the fact that most regimes are likely to have at least some minimal administrative apparatus for dispute settlement, collection and sharing of information or surveillance. The scope of the regimes refers to the range of sub-issues the regime covers. Finally, the nature of the issue area and the extent of cooperation sought by a given regime will partly determine the preferences for market-oriented issues authoritative modes of allocation by the regimes. Any perceptible change in any of these four aspects will invariably bring consequent alterations in the domain of the regime concerned.

We may now, in conclusion, identify the merits of the Regime approach developed in the USA. First, the focus of regimes is neither as broad as the international structure, nor as narrow as the study of formal organizations. Secondly, there has been a rudimentary reconciliation of the idealist and realist traditions, assuming that patterns of state action are influenced by norms, but such norm-governed behaviour is wholly consistent with the pursuit of national interests. Thirdly, this theory has accepted tension areas in inter-state relations, to an extent natural and permissible, after which there commences erosion of the regime built. Fourthly, the central aspects of all theoretical approaches to international cooperations (i.e. organization, functional collaboration, supranationality, from economic to political integration through 'spilling,' etc.) have been taken cognizance of. Fifthly, the theory of hegemonic stability (a structural explanation of regimes) views that actual international relations leading to the emergence of a hegemon in a region can also bring about stability and order in that region by procuring the consent of the weaker states in favour of security and/or economic regime built by the hegemon. This may be seen, at least partially, in many real-life situations of many Third World regions. Finally, the domestic socio-political factor is also being accepted as a variable in regime constructions and evaluations, which makes the International Regime Theory further realistic and broadly applicable.

This, then, sets forth the overview of the American theoretical construct regarding the International Regime Theory which we shall seek to apply now in the case of the nuclear non-proliferation issue.

Critique of the Existing Nuclear Non-Proliferation Regime (NPR)

The singlemost sensitive issue in the post Second World War which has invited the maximum debates and controversies has been undoubtedly the nuclear issue. Applying the regime model in the case of the existing NPR, we can identify its basic causal factors, nature of regime and its outcomes—as outlined in the figure on the next page. In this figure, we have also identified the several instruments and devices developed by the NPR to institutionalise itself and these devices are critically outlined below.

We can first refer to the theory of nuclear deterrence which depicts a balance if terror or mutually assured destruction (MAD) among the Nuclear Weapons States (NWS) which is capable enough to deter any possible nuclear holocaust, protect the allies and ordain global peace and stability. Deterrence means discouraging the enemy from taking military actions by posing for him a prospect of cost and risk sufficient to outweigh his prospective gain. Today credibility in nuclear deterrence is getting eroded with an improved understanding that once the first few shots are exchanged, it may not be possible to exercise effective command and control over a nuclear weapons exchange and prevent its rapid escalation. Moreover, the very possession of N-weapons is increasingly considered to be unethical, as against the ethics of deterrence which denounces the threat or use of the weapon, not its possession. Finally, the ill-fated logic of 'infinite proliferation for perpetual peace' or chain reaction syndrome, a core factor in deterrence, has led to a dismal scenario today.

A central instrument of the NPR, is the Non-Proliferation Treaty (NPT), signed in 1968 and effective from 1970. Its more important provisions are outlined below:

Art I: prohibits transfer of nuclear weapons and nuclear explosive devices;

Art II: prohibits NNWS (non-nuclear weapons states) to receive them;

Existing Nuclear Non-Proliferation Regime (NPR)

BASIC CAUSAL FACTORS

1) *Egoistic Self-interest*
[to maintain super/major-power status for the powerful sponsors of the regime]

2) *Political Power*
[to monopolise jointly the power accuring from nuclear and missile technology and use it as a means of coercing, cajoling and trade with NNWS]

3) *Norms and Principles*
[selective possession of this special power in the hands of the NWS who can 'ordain' the world to order and 'protect' their allies]

4) *Habits and Customs*
[acceptance of the safeguards, as those of the IAEA, vigilance over the 'threshold' states, limitations over and non-nuclear cooperation with the NNWS]; and

5) *Knowledge*
[monopoly over the concerned technical know-how and restrict its horizontal and spatial dispersion].

Negotiated among NWS and Imposed over NNWS

Nature of the regime created:

(1) *Structural aspect:*
—Establish the hegemony of the major NWS

(2) *Functional aspect:*
—zealously guard the monopoly of the NWS over the concerned nuclear/missile technology and assist the NNWS in non-nuclear functional fields as a positive deterrent;

(3) *Cognitive aspect*
—seek to extract the hegemony of the NWS.

RELATED PATTERNED BEHAVIOUR AND OUTCOME

(1) *POSITIVE*
—Perceptible control of quick/unbridled vertical, spatial and horizontal proliferation, mainly due to many signatories.

(2) *NEGATIVE*
(stronger outcome)
—a skewed, partial and unsuccessful regime;
—'threshold' states outside;
—several violations by the major signatories themselves.

NPR

a) RULE/ THEORY	(b) DECISIONS/ ARRANGEMENTS	(c) INSTITUTIONS	(d) PROCEDURES
Nuclear Deterrence Mutually Assured Destruction Discriminate Deterrence	Nuclear Non-Proliferation Treaty (NPT) Missile Technology Control Regime (MTCR) Nuclear Weapons Free Zone (NWFZ)	mainly, International Atomic Energy Agency (IAEA)	(tacit/implicit) nuclear blackmailing tied aid diplomacy arms trade technology transfer conditional political support espionage and media use

Art III: prohibits providing source of special fissionable materials, or equipments specially designed for processing, use or production of special fissionable materials to any NNWS even for peaceful purposes, without subjecting them to safeguards;
Art IV: offers technology to NNWS with respect to nuclear power-generation (as a bargaining point);
Art VI: calls for early negotiations for nuclear disarmament under effective international control;
Art VII: provides for the amendment of the NPT;
Art VIII: calls for a review conference at Geneva after every 5 years.
Art X: provides for a conference after 25 years (i.e. 1995) to decide on the status of the treaty in future.

The advocates of the NPT opine that the proliferation of decision making centres of nuclear weapons enhances the dangers of a nuclear war and, hence, restraints in these centres are required. They also hold that in spite of the incentive of nations with reasonable scientific and industrial infrastructure to go nuclear, the pace of proliferation has been very slow due to NPT.

However, the very fact that nations representing 45% of world's population were yet non-signatories of the NPT until recently is a telling illustration of its incompatibility. The seven important non-signatory NWS and 'threshold' states are: France (NWS), India (test done), Israel (sophisticated nuclear raw materials arsenal), Pakistan (advanced stage of research), Argentina and Brazil (fissile materials production capabilities) and South Africa (clandestine nuclear weapons efforts on). China has recently signed the NPT, only in 1992. NPT led NWS to monopolise hegemonistic instruments of mass destruction. It objects to horizontal proliferation in NNWS, but 'allows' vertical and spatial proliferation by the NWS.

In the 1980s, the major NWS have been attempting to control the spread of nuclear technology by controlling the delivery systems through MTCR (Missile Technology Control Regime), joined by 7 industrialised nations in April 1988 (later also joined by USSR in 1989). 'Selectivity' was specifically mentioned in the new arrangements and controls were programmed to be applied in case of 'suspects missile programme.' Israel, South Africa and

Pakistan were exempted from the agreement. A concept developed in 1980s—Discriminate Deterrence—should be viewed in contrast with MTCR. While the MTCR aims to prevent the Third World nations from acquiring ballistic missiles and would nullify their ability to retaliate, Discriminate Deterrence calls for use/deployment of long-range, high-tech smart missile systems against the Third World nations and enhances the capability of the NWS to employ the threat of the use of nuclear force in developing regions.

NWFZ (Nuclear Weapons Free Zone) has been an arrangement professed mainly by the Third World and advocated to be incorporated in the existing NPR; but this has not normally found favours with the West. The Tlatelelco Treaty, seeking to establish an NWFZ in Latin America, does not cover more than 50% of the continent, including Argentina, Brazil, Chile or Cuba. Also the US's contingent plans to bring nuclear depth charges to the Roosevelt Road in Puerto Rico during hostilities, kills the spirit of this NWFZ.

Western powers have refused to recognize the Raro-tonga Treaty seeking to establish an NWFZ in the Asia-Pacific region. Due to the American bases in the Subic Bay or the Clark Airfield, USA has also discouraged the idea of South-East Asian NWFZ. Palme Commission's proposal of nuclear free Central European Corridor, or proposals of NWFZ in Nordic, Artic and Balkan areas, have also not found favours with the West. The US Report on Discriminate Deterrence stresses the need for very low yield highly accurate weapons (not excluding nuclear warheads) for possible use in future wars, thus making a mockery of the NWFZs.

A host of tacit and implicit procedures are utilised by the US led West to internalise its NPR within the Third World. The most controversial procedure has been that of nuclear blackmailing. NWS use nuclear weapons as a threat-phenomenon to achieve their goals or protect their allies in the Third World, and till December 1988, there have been at least 41 such threats.

Coercive nuclear diplomacy by the US or the UK has been seen in Korea (1950), Quemoy-Matsu (1953), Enterprises incident (1971) of Falklands Crisis (1982). The vulnerability of the

NNWS is exposed by the fact that spatial proliferation, bases, early warning facilities, and related infrastructure in the Third World are continued unabated by the NWS in exchange of aid, loan, investment, threats and protection. Thus, ironically, the Third World provides for the priority targets for a decapacitating strike in case of a strategic nuclear exchange between the NWS. We find no comprehensive security guarantee been given to the NNWS against the threat of the use of nuclear weapons, in exchange of their renunciation of the nuclear option. Further, the NATO-allies profess the nuclear deterrence or 'flexible response' concept, but oppose 'no-first-use' doctrine, accepted by the erstwhile USSR and the PRC. This option is thus kept open by the NATO for effective nuclear blackmailing.

Finally, we can further substantiate the evident unsuccessful nature of the existing NPR by the compromises and violations made by both—the signatories and non-signatories of the NPT. First due to overt and covert violations by the big signatories, nuclear weapons storage, command, control, communication and intelligence facilities have spread over at least 62 nations and territories; and all oceans except perhaps Antarctica, have naval vessels with nuclear weapons deployed.

Secondly, new nuclear 'concepts' and practices have been devised by the major signatories which are blatant violations of the existing NPR—like modernisation of current nuclear arsenals both at the strategic levels (e.g. USA's Peace-keeper, Midgetman, Trident D-5, air and sea launched cruise missiles, and their analogous systems on the Soviet side), and tactical levels extending the ranges and accuracy of nuclear weapons to gain a capability to implement a doctrine of discriminate deterrence. Also reference can be made to the extension of weaponisation into outer space through the 'Star Wars' programme at the USA.

Thirdly, trafficking in fissile materials provides another blatant violation of the existing NPR. For example, Israel has diverted fissile materials from the NUMEC plant, Apollo, Penn of the USA, has hijacked the ship, Sheerberg, with Uranium cargo. The German firm NUKEM is under investigation for exporting to Pakistan nuclear waste materials containing plutonium. Iran and Iraq, both signatories of the NPT, have been engaged in the acquisition of weapons grade fissile materials from a black market based in Khartoum, Sudan. Argentina has procured weapons grade Uranium from West Germany in 1985. Thousands of pounds of plutonium were unaccounted for at 15 commercial plants regulated by the US Atomic Energy Commission.

Fourthly, a serious study is required to analyse the impact of the proliferation of nuclear propelled submarines on international naval strategic doctrines. The erstwhile USSR has transferred a Victor class nuclear propelled submarine to India. The US government has agreed to transfer technology to build nuclear propelled submarines for the Canadian government, and the UK has made a bid for the contract. But the reactors on the nuclear propelled submarines and their needed technology cannot be for peaceful purposes. Thus Articles I, II and VI of the NPT have been repeatedly breached in practice even by the major signatories, and a nuclear propelled submarine can sail through Art. III. Also, Art. IV on nuclear power generation/station has been rendered obsolete in the light of the Three Mile Island and Chernobyl accidents. Need there be said anything about the fate of NPT—today and tomorrow?

Alternative Scheme for a Nuclear Elimination Regime

Given this situation, there is a two-pronged approach towards modifying the existing NPR: the reformist or incrementalist approach and the radicalist approach. For example as a reformist modification, strategists like Pierre Gallois and Kenneth Waltz have professed the limitation of 'legal' proliferation within the three declared signatories and the eight capable non-signatories. But this is also a skewed scheme.

Another reformist approach calls for a revision of NPT by making nuclear weapons impotent, reducing stockpiles, decaying the doctrine of Nuclear Deterrence over time (say by 1995), and a new treaty akin to UNCLOS to be signed with all important states participating. The Pugwash Council has already been operating on a project for a reformed regime—to initiate interaction among the concerned nations on the role of nuclear weapons in the current IR, on nuclear strategic doctrines and their feasibility, the role of war in the industrialised world, and the motivations of nations to go nuclear.

The last two approaches may pave the way for the emergence of the radicalist view of total denuclearization (already suggested by the PM Rajiv Gandhi in 1988) or a nuclear elimination regime. This is very much essential because the entire exercise of 'controlling' proliferation is rendered futile when we observe that every nuclear submarine constitutes an independent decision making centre—and, hence security, in a world of limited and controlled proliferation also, is rendered hazardous.

However, we would prefer an all-out denuclearization, even in the context of the so-called 'peaceful' uses of the nuclear power, for several reasons, a few important ones being mentioned.

First, nuclear power is limited by uranium availability and its 70% contribution to our energy requirements would mean that all known uranium supplies would be exhausted by 2011 AD.

Secondly, 40 years of research on the theoretically fuel efficient fast breeder reactors (FBRs) has failed to produce a single viable design; and even if there is a breakthrough, an expanded nuclear programme would run out of uranium fuel before the breeders can be brought into use.

Thirdly, global warming, in near future, may itself make nuclear power generation impossible since more extreme variations of temperature are predicted.

Fourthly, large quantities of energy are used in uranium mining and its enriching processes, in fabricating fuel-rods, in heavy water production, and in cooling spent fuel, decommissioned reactors and highly radioactive wastes; and hence, the net energy obtainable would be much lower than assumed and may even be negative.

Fifthly, as for the costs, in the UK today, the cost of electricity from nuclear power is 7 to 10 pence per kilowatt as compared to one penny for that from natural gas. Also, since nuclear power is heavily subsidised by all governments, it appears to be feasible and cheap.

Sixthly, with Chernobyl, nuclear energy will never be a paying proposition since it has been estimated to cause 40,000 victims altogether, and the cost of the cleanup in 1986 itself was over 4 billion, not including the cost of extra deaths and the mental anguish of thousands of people exposed to the fallout radiation, nor the expenses incurred by the other nations.

Seventhly, nuclear power does contribute to a sizeable CO2 pollution; and a 1000 MW station has been calculated to contribute about 2,30,000 tonnes of CO2 per year.

Eighthly, the safe disposal of nuclear reactor wastes has proved to be an insurmountable problem although reactors have been in use for most of this century. In this context, neither the storage of wastes can justifiably be a global problem, nor having storage sites ensures that the storage methods will be safe for the posterity, when still the radioactive wastes will remain hazardous. Exposure to excess radiation could lead to genetic mutations being inherited and mutations in micro-organisms.

Ninthly, the plutonium obtained from processing spent fuel, is highly radioactive.

Finally, the experience of the industrialized countries has also revealed the vulnerabilities in current nuclear power plants which were not fully understood when the plants were designed. Among the most important are human error, materials degradation, accidents, resulting from chains of subtle failures and the economic sensitivity of nuclear projects to disruption and poor workmanship.

Thus, there can be a meaningful non-proliferation of nuclear weapons only if there is a non-proliferation of nuclear reactors, which will lead to the elimination of the reactors, and thereby of nuclear power, totally.

We are now at the historic threshold of a new era which shall dawn an alternative nuclear elimination regime, with its new set of basic causal factors; process and nature of the regimes; theory, institutions, decisions and procedures of the regime; and outcomes of the regimes.

Research Scholar
University of Bombay